The Family Game

Identities for Young & Old

The Family Game

Identities for Young & Old

by William Braden

Quadrangle

A New York Times Company

THE FAMILY GAME

This book was commissioned by public television station WQED in Pittsburgh to accompany "The Family Game," a series of twelve television programs.

Cover design and illustrations: Ed Zelinsky
Copy Editor: Joyce Cherones
Design Coordinator: Roger Schneider

Library of Congress Card Number: 72-89854

ISBN: 0-8129-6205-2

BOOK TITLE: The Family Game

Contents

To Elsie Brittain and H. Wheeler Brittain

Foreword

About a year ago, WQED, the public television station in Pittsburgh, was scratching about to find an effective way to do a new series of programs. The station had just completed a nationwide series on drug abuse called *The Turned On Crisis,* which had done very well. It had won The Community Service Award from the Corporation for Public Broadcasting and then The George Foster Peabody Award. Both high honors and, on the strength of them, the Corporation asked WQED to do another group of national programs on the circumstances that gave rise to the drug culture. Specifically, The Corporation was interested in an investigation of what was then known as The Generation Gap. That is where the problem began.

The difficulty was that the gap was hard to find. It had either been closed or somehow mislaid. The revolutionary movement so evident a short time before —with its promises of new life styles, altered consciousness, political realignments, and cultural experiment—had faded away. The only remaining traces were the Levis and long hair of the young, the sideburns of advertising executives, and an occasional and distant cry from Abbie Hoffman or some other prophet who had been abandoned on a hillside. Americans, young and old, seemed wrapped in a quiet confusion.

All this was disappointing to the producers at WQED. The clear-cut, jab-and-thrust conflicts between generations were no longer available. Documentary films on anti-social acts of the young and encounter sessions with parents revealing guilts and fears could not be programmed. It seemed that public television had arrived on the parade grounds too late; the bands had already taken off their uniforms and gone home.

Yet, in many ways, it was a good time to arrive. In that quiet moment it was possible to consider some necessary questions. Had the youth movement been enlarged beyond reasonable proportions? Was the cleft between generations as severe as television newscasts and books by Kenneth Keniston often made it appear? There had been plenty of radical ideas and dramatic events, but what impression had they made? These questions prompted others and eventually determined the structure of WQED's television programs.

The series became an inquiry into family matters. What happens between fathers and sons, how is the mother's role defined, are there new ways to organize a family—in short, questions about generations were followed to their primal level. The series is called *The Family Game* because, despite all the questions, firm answers are not supplied. The game consists in noting the moves people make—the way they argue, the pressures they encounter—but no winners are selected. The viewers are asked to decide that or, at least, discuss what they have seen. It is WQED's version of participating television and a much livelier programming idea than the one originally projected. Arriving late has its benefits.

Still, the series had to do more than stir troubled water and then run for cover. It had some responsibility to suggest a point of perspective. That is the reason this book was commissioned.

I was the WQED producer who finally put the series together and, while preparing for that task, I read William Braden's book, *The Age of Aquarius*. It was a careful attempt to analyze the youth movement from multiple viewpoints and I found it most helpful as a guide for organizing the television materials. I asked Braden if we could meet and, when we did, two things emerged from our conversation. The first was that he verified the impression given by other authorities who were consulted on the series; nearly everyone was confused about the current status of the relationships between old and young in America. The second was that he was just the man to write a book to accompany our television programs.

When we met, Braden was busily preparing a series of articles later published in *The Chicago Sun-Times* on the same general areas we were exploring on television. He was making the rounds of campuses and factories and interviewing men of opinion throughout the country. He was prepared to report on the broad currents of concern among young people and their parents. His was the informed overview.

The television series was to move at a more intense and personal level. People of varying ages, races, and social conditions were gathered in groups and asked to discuss and dramatize their responses to questions that affect the family. This process produced a line of intimate dramas which parallel Braden's discussion of the larger themes.

This is the correspondence we have tried to maintain between the television series and the book. It does not always work and we haven't worried much about that. For example, the television program on communes concentrates upon alternate forms of family life, a point that Braden discusses in his related chapter, but he then focuses his attention upon the rejection of technology that is part of the communal idea. So it goes throughout. The Braden *Family Game* frequently plays on a much larger and more abstract level than the television series. The changes of emphasis are natural since, from the start, we assumed that the two units would not duplicate each other but have a complementary connection. The television program gives emotional clarification to a situation which the book enlarges, defines, and relates to other areas of attention.

However, that interplay is not of immediate importance. The book makes its own coherence. We have included excerpts from the television series before each chapter by which a reader may recall programs he has seen and also have specific examples of the attitudes Braden discusses. Still, the book belongs to Braden and I am pleased that the television series has provided the opportunity for bringing it into print.

John Sommers
Executive Producer
THE FAMILY SERIES
WQED, Pittsburgh

Author's Note

Who am I? What are my credentials? By what authority am I qualified to write a book covering such a broad range of subjects—literally from Anarchy to Zen?

I am a newspaper reporter. Since 1956, I have been a general-assignment reporter for the *Chicago Sun-Times,* and in that capacity I have covered stories from the Death of God to the death of a President—from radical theology to the funeral of John F. Kennedy. That means I do not have a specific beat and makes me, I suppose, more or less a professional generalist, although one book reviewer (in the *London Times* literary supplement) has described me as a reporter whose beat is the history of ideas. That's very elegant, although I must confess I also cover fires, shootings, and ribbon cutting ceremonies.

I have written two previous books: *The Private Sea,* a study of theology and psychedelic drug mysticism, and *The Age of Aquarius,* a study of technology and the youth counterculture. Both of those books grew out of newspaper assignments and so did *The Family Game.* In this case, I was assigned by James F. Hoge, Jr., editor of the *Sun-Times,* to examine the "new mood" on America's college and university campuses and, as an aspect of that, the apparent demise of the radical political Movement.

I was given six months to tour the country and research the subject, and, in doing so, I talked to hundreds of young people, academicians, political activists and social critics. The result was a series of articles published in the *Sun-Times* at the end of the last academic year. *The Family Game* is to some degree an extension of those articles, and I thank the *Sun-Times* for its permission to incorporate relevant sections from the articles in the following pages. In writing the book, I also in a few cases drew on pertinent interviews in *The Age of Aquarius*. But most of *The Family Game* consists of fresh material, and each of its ten essays was written to relate specifically to the programs in the television series produced by WQED for The Public Broadcasting Service.

The essays also are intended primarily to offer questions rather than answers and to provide at least a general overview of the many conflicting opinions provoked by those questions—to describe, in other words, the spectrum of debate involved in various social issues.

My approach both to newspaper reporting and book writing has been to read the relevant literature and then, whenever possible, to consult the oracles themselves; to interview the authorities—the people who wrote the literature —and to draw them out further, for example, by asking Expert A his opinion of Expert B. I would then bring their comments and reactions together within the covers of a single book, letting them speak for themselves, and encouraging the reader to form his own conclusions. Having reported a thesis and anti-thesis, I might sometimes suggest a possible synthesis. But for the most part, in my previous books, I would maintain the stance of the objective and disinterested newspaperman who reports rather than comments, and whose main purpose is to stimulate thought and discussion, not to set people straight. Somebody once said that the author's essential message in virtually every book is "Why can't you be more like me?" and I have always tried to avoid that conceit. While I still oppose the subjective New Journalism in newspaper reporting, however, in *The Family Game* I do occasionally toss aside my press card and speak my own mind—partly because I do have personal convictions regarding some of the subjects discussed, partly to be provocative, and partly because, after devoting years to trend-spotting, I have frankly grown a bit weary of the intellectual quarterbacks calling an audible every time we reach the line of scrimmage.

Even so, I still believe it is my basic function to serve as a reporter; I feel quite humble about my capacity to comment with authority on so many complex issues. My appreciation of complexity grows by the day, and I am increasingly convinced, along with Wallace Stevens, that "the squirming facts exceed the squamous mind."

I still would rather listen than speak, and at this point, I would like to thank at least a few of the people whose comments in recent interviews and conversations contributed significantly to this book:

Saul Alinsky, R. Stephen Berry, Kenneth Boulding, Farrel Broslawsky, Joseph Bute, Nicole Dreiske, Daniel X. Freedman, Patrick J. Glynn, III, Andrew M. Greeley, Edward T. Hall, Michael Harrington, Sidney Hyman, Irving Levine, Martin E. Marty, Peter Max, Daniel Offer, Martin Peretz, B. F. Skinner, Kevin Starr, Howard Stein, Michael Wadleigh, and Hayden White.

Saul Alinsky died while this book was being written, and I offer him this tribute which he would understand and, I know, appreciate: Saul Alinsky, too, was "something of a man."

For earlier talks which provided important insights that are reflected again in this book, my thanks once more to Thomas J. J. Altizer, Bruno Bettelheim, Jarl E. Dyrud, Erik H. Erikson, Fred Hampton, Kenneth Kenniston, Christopher Lasch, Timothy Leary, Milton W. Monson, Jr., and Joseph J. Schwab.

Finally, in deepest gratitude for their support in what for me were very dark days, I thank editor James F. Hoge, Jr., managing editor Ralph Otwell, and city editor Jim Peneff of the *Chicago Sun-Times*.

William Braden
Chicago/1972

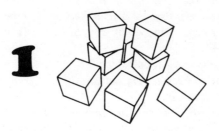

The final program of the television series brings together Gary, a young follower of the counter-culture, and Izzy, a middle-aged metallurgist. Gary has a beard and long, curly hair, and Izzy sits eying him carefully.

Gary:	*Well?*
Izzy:	*I can look at you all day long. It doesn't make me happy. It sure doesn't.*
Gary:	*What's wrong?*
Izzy:	*Nothing's wrong. It just doesn't make me happy.*
Gary:	*I don't wish you had long hair. What's it do to you?*
Izzy:	*It stopped upsetting me after I compromised and that's one of the hallmarks of my generation is that we're willing to compromise with reality. I can't do anything about it. I'm not gonna upset myself with it. And I don't. However, I don't have to like it.*
Gary:	*You really don't want to touch me.*
Izzy:	*I don't. You know why? Your whole appearance, your whole lifestyle offends me.*
Gary:	*I'm ugly?*
Izzy:	*You're not ugly. You're better looking than me. However you sure have tried very hard to make yourself ugly. The fact is you have absolutely succeeded. There is no question about it. You don't seem to know where you're going and how you're going to get there . . .*
Gary:	*I'm not trying to go anywhere.*
Izzy:	*I don't understand that.*
Gary:	*It's very simple. All I am is what I am now. I try not to be a bunch of memories, a bunch of yesterdays, or a thing anticipating tomorrow. I'm just trying to function in the present, to*

just accept things for the moment as they are.

Izzy: *What are you contributing to this world, functioning this way? Don't you want to be a contributing member of the world? You're functioning day by day, but what is your purpose and function?*

Gary: *To breathe and eat and sleep.*

Izzy: *That's it? That's a very selfish attitude. You're only contributing to yourself.*

Gary: *Well, selfish, you can say that because you see a difference between you and me. I don't see a difference. I see a oneness between all of us. I feel like you're just extensions. Like, I feel the space between us is made of the same atoms that you and I are made of . . .*

Izzy: *That's just an empty rationalization. I still believe that the way to change things is through the ballot box. I know that's a very old-fashioned concept, however . . .*

Gary: *But the ballot box is one of the first things that screwed up everything.*

Izzy: *That's ridiculous. They just gave the vote to the 18-year-old. Now, if you ever had the opportunity, your generation, to do something, this is the time to do it. If you don't believe in the system or you don't believe the way the system is run, you can help to change the system.*

Gary: *How do you think we got the vote?*

Izzy: *I figured it was about time . . .*

Gary: *You think Nixon said, "Let's give these kids the vote"? Like we got the vote by going out and doin' things . . .*

Izzy: *By demonstrating?*

Gary: *By standing up and asking for it. Yes, by demonstrations . . .*

Izzy: *By running around the White House?*

Gary: *O.K.*

Izzy: *By standing on the hill and in front of the Lincoln Memorial?*

Gary: *That's right.*

Izzy: *You did. You made an impression whether you like it or not. You made an impression.*

Gary: *You think it was good then that we demonstrated?*

Izzy: *No, I didn't say I thought it was good. I think it was effective. Now everybody says, for example, that I don't at my age understand you. But I'll tell you something. You show less understanding of me than I ever think I have shown of your generation.*

Gary: *I can't fathom you at all. You're right. I can't get to where* *you're at.*

Izzy: *I don't want for you to be where I'm at. I'd like for you to understand how I am, what I am, and what made what I am. That's all I ask you. I don't ask you to like me. I don't even ask you to agree with me. The fact is I would be very happy if you don't agree with me.*

Gary: *Why?*

Izzy: *Because I don't agree with you.*

1.
The Youthquake

In 1960, the torch was passed to a new generation of Americans. They dropped it.

After more than a decade of protest, the youthful vision of a transformed society has faded like the cloud-capped towers of Camelot. Hippies, Yippies, and Weathermen—these actors in the revolutionary drama, their revels ended, are spirits melted into air. Serious adult political activists have rubbed the fairy dust from their eyes and have abandoned the college campus as their radical power base. The youth counterculture also has experienced a sea change, and consciousness elevation is no longer promoted as a substitute for structural reform.

These developments were widely reported during the 1971-72 academic year, when the national press administered last rites to the radical coalition referred to as the Movement. What the media giveth, the media taketh away.

In retrospect, it is obvious now that the degree of youthful commitment to the Movement was tremendously distorted by the media, the public, and the young people themselves; that much of it was inspired by peer pressure rather than ideological conviction; that many of the young were into it essentially for therapy; that the concept of a generation gap was largely a myth. But the 1960s appeared at the time to be a decade of significant generational conflict which threatened to destroy the nation's political institutions and the foundations of the American family. It is important to understand the complex factors that created that impression, and the subject can be explored at many levels. This introductory chapter will review the history of the 1960s and early 1970s from a political perspective.

To begin, turn back the clock to 1954.

That was the year the U.S. Supreme Court handed down the Brown decision banning racial segregation in schools, which laid the basis for the major domestic dispute of the 1960s. It was the year of the French defeat at Dienbienphu and the Geneva agreements, which laid the basis for the major foreign-policy dispute of the 1960s. And it was the year Allen Ginsberg discovered Zen, publishing his poem "Howl," which marked the beginning of the West Coast beatnik influence and which laid the basis for the so-called Leap to the East that was later to be incorporated in the 1960s counter-culture.

Thus the tinder was provided for the conflagrations of the decade to follow. But only a superficial analysis would suggest a simple cause and effect relationship in this situation, which occurred of course within a much broader historical context of immigration, urbanization, technological development, social upheaval—and half a century of war, depression, war, and cold war.

The young people of the 1950s were known as the silent generation, and this reporter was one of the deaf and dumb members. It remains to be asked just why we were so silent, and why the adult population appeared to be equally mute.

For one thing, we were relatively few in number as a result of the low depression birthrate. We also bore the psychological scars of the depression, which tended to make us security-oriented, and many of us were married veterans with family responsibilities. The country as a whole was resting after its wartime exertions. Beyond this, however, there had been an unprecedented interruption of historical continuity: a traumatic break in the American tradition of political dissent from the left. And the personification of this phenomenon was Senator Joseph R. McCarthy, who had charged in 1950 that the U. S. State Department was infiltrated with Communists.

It would be difficult to overestimate the impact of McCarthyism in shaping the character of dissent in the 1960s.

Waving a list of names he wouldn't show to anybody (including my *Chicago Sun-Times* colleague Irv Kupcinet, who confronted him on the spot and challenged him to read it), McCarthy virtually destroyed the adult left. McCarthy as an individual, of course, could not have created such havoc had it not been for the situation he set out to exploit: namely, our sudden global involvement in a cold war with Russia, and the fact that a generation of leftists had been previously involved in various permutations of Marxist ideology. The shade of red didn't matter. Democratic socialists, New Deal reformers, Progressive Party supporters—with few exceptions, that entire generation confessed its sins and fled from the political stage.

But by 1960, a new cast of characters had gathered in the wings and was waiting for its cue.

The currents that produce historical change flow at a subterranean level, where they often are impossible to detect, and during the 1950s there had been at least two such undercurrents developing—one of them demographic, the other economic. The postwar baby explosion had been crowding elementary and high schools with millions of young people who were destined to become the Now Generation: what *Time* magazine would later describe as "the youthquake." And postwar affluence had provided middle-class parents with the income to bankroll their children to a college education. Also, the first Russian Sputnik in 1957 had produced the impression of a brain gap and contributed to the conviction that all those children should go to college whether they wanted to or not, that the mass production of Ph.D.s was a national priority.

So colleges in the 1960s were hit by a shock wave of students, many of whom would normally have gone directly into the work force and psychosocial adulthood. With their parents paying the bills, the students had plenty of leisure time on their hands; they also had a unique opportunity to function as external critics of the society that had not yet admitted them to full membership. As late as 1959, however, they were otherwise occupied: stuffing themselves into telephone booths.

This has since been attributed, in large part, to the presence in the White House of Dwight David Eisenhower.

Ironically, many radicals today appear to have developed a rather curious nostalgia for Eisenhower. After all, he did pull us out of one Asian war and refused to embroil us in another one, rejecting the suggestion of his vice president that we rescue the French after the fall of the Dienbienphu fortress. As a general who hated war but knew the business, he was ideally suited to deal with the Pentagon; he thus created an alleged missile gap that was later found to be illusory. And it was Eisenhower in his farewell address who warned the nation about the menace he described as the military-industrial complex.

His critics point out that he failed to do anything about McCarthy, who was finally done in by television exposure which revealed the senator as a bully and blew his cover as the guy in the white hat. It has been said, in fact, that Eisenhower failed to do anything about anything during his two terms, and indeed one of the jokes from that period was the Eisenhower doll (you wind it up and it does nothing for eight years). But it is precisely this quality that is now represented as the late President's cardinal virtue.

"He maybe did nothing to reduce our burdens," said social scientist Martin Peretz, an expert on the McCarthy era. "On the other hand, he didn't add to our burdens. And he didn't promise us anything. Believe in the old verities, he told us, and let's muddle through."

Then came 1960, and the election of John F. Kennedy.

"Remember that famous line in the inaugural?" said Peretz. " 'Ask not what your country can do for you, ask what you can do for your country.' That absolutely drove me wacky. I know it sounded great to a lot of people, but it reminded me at the time of those signs they have outside Spanish police stations: *'Toda Para Patria.'* I mean, people's lives aren't meant for the national service, are they? I always thought the nation was meant for people."

More to the point, Kennedy addressed himself repeatedly to the "new generation of Americans." Passing them the torch, he reminded them that they were the heirs of the first revolution, and that "each generation of Americans has been summoned to give testimony to its national loyalty." He asked them to join in a historic effort, to assure a more fruitful life for all mankind. He told them that man held in his mortal hands the power to abolish all forms of human poverty. And he urged them: "Together let us explore the stars, conquer the deserts, eradicate disease, tap the ocean depths, and encourage the arts and commerce."

Whereas Eisenhower promised nothing, and raised no expectations, Kennedy promised movement on every conceivable front. But if Kennedy's rhetoric made young people feel they could make the world anew, they were not provided with any guidelines for accomplishing this heroic project—a consequence, as already indicated, of the deauthorization of the Old Left during the McCarthy period.

"My generation should have been there," said community organizer Saul Alinsky. "When I was developing as a radical at the University of Chicago, I had guys like Clarence Darrow who'd invite me over to his home on a Sunday afternoon, and I'd sit on the floor and look up at him like he was God. I had John L. Lewis and top CIO organizers and socialists and Communists. I had people all over the place—good people, wonderful people, fighting people. But all the guys from my generation—when Joe McCarthy got loose, they took off for the woodwork. So when this new generation came around, this SDS generation, there were only two guys over 25 they'd even listen to: myself and Paul Goodman."

"There was no intermediate generation," agreed Michael Harrington, national chairman of the Socialist Party. "You could go back to the 1820s, if you wanted to get fancy about it, and there had always been new and fairly large generations of the left. But the left in the 1950s had been cut down to a ridiculous handful.

"I was in Port Huron in 1962, when they drafted the SDS [Students for a Democratic Society] manifesto, and I argued with them on two issues. For one thing, they were tending toward the point of view that the enemy of my enemy is my friend: because communism is anticapitalist, it's good. And I tried to say that's not true at all. More important, they came up with the theory all liberals were a bunch of sellouts. And once they assumed that—

once they assumed that Walter Reuther was a fink, which they very explicitly did, even when they were trying to get money out of Reuther—where were they going to go? They had destroyed all the mass possibilities.

"So these kids all thought they were starting out de novo. And at that point, as a result, they were antitheoretical. My phrase for the speaking style that was typical in SDS then is the stutter-style. They were suspicious of anybody who was smooth; they were suspicious of anybody who could quote Marx. So one thing was, they had no sense of dialectical complexity—that liberalism had been both good and bad and had both good and bad elements —because they had no adults who could tutor them in these very complicated kind of things. And they adopted a sort of moralistic, straight-forward approach."

If the young were antitheoretical, the academic line at the start of the 1960s was anti-ideological. The sociologist Daniel Bell and others had declared an End of Ideology, asserting that intellectuals and workers alike had reached a rough consensus on political issues that precluded any further debate on alternative economic and social structures. Predictions of inevitable class warfare had failed to prove true in highly industrialized societies, it was said, and America had achieved a stable system in which there was general agreement on national goals and the functions of the welfare state. Old Left intellectuals were united in a common front against the cold war enemy, and their approach to domestic social issues was a pragmatic emphasis on increased production: on continued growth of the Gross National Product to provide enough jobs and goods for all Americans. The Kennedy administration likewise contributed to the impression that the operations of government could be entrusted to an elite corps of efficient, problem-solving social managers.

Reaction to the Cuban invasion of 1961 did provide the nucleus for an ideological wing in SDS, and enchantment with Kennedy as a politican was seldom expressed in that organization. But the cadences of the 1962 Port Huron manifesto are remarkably similar to those of the Kennedy inaugural. And the content of the manifesto was essentially an idealistic, moral statement within the American frame of reference. It was not an attack on the nation's institutions but an ethical demand that the nation live up to its own ideals.

The SDS in any case never represented more than a tiny fraction of the total youth movement. What Kennedy had done for young people in general was to legitimize idealism. And it was moral idealism that inspired most youthful protest from the start of the decade until 1968, when that inspiration died in the streets of Chicago.

"It wasn't very complicated," said a Harvard graduate student, reflecting on those days. "We simply accepted all of the American house clichés, and decided to make them work."

The downing of the U-2 spy plane in Russia in 1960 probably caused the first shock of recognition that ended the myth of American innocence abroad, and Cuba was the second such trauma. But there was as yet no clearly defined issue involving the conduct of our foreign policy, and indeed the newly formed Peace Corps offered an opportunity to exercise moral enthusiasm doing good works overseas. On the domestic front, however, there was an issue that came into sharp focus when black students conducted the first lunchcounter sit-in early in 1960 in Greensboro, N. C. So the white students joined the civil rights movement. And that remained their major form of social commitment until the blacks went their separate ways in the middle of the decade.

Dissolution of the civil rights coalition very neatly coincided with the first serious eruption of campus protest: with the Free Speech Movement at the University of California at Berkeley in the fall of 1964.

Berkeley students had been involved in a 1960 demonstration against the House Un-American Activities Committee in San Francisco. But the campus itself had been calm, Vietnam was not yet an issue, and the FSM marked a new departure: a protest directed against the university as an institution. The immediate cause of the protest was the administration's decision to enforce an old rule prohibiting political groups from passing out literature on campus property; but the grievance was expanded to include a condemnation of the quality of life in general, and especially the life of students in the impersonal atmosphere of the multiversity. It was Berkeley students who first voiced the slogan: "I am a human being. Do not fold, spindle or mutilate."

Setting a precedent for future error, authorities called in the cops. Thus it began.

And gradually it escalated. But very gradually. And the wonder now— looking back on it—is how long the students persisted in their idealistic effort to change society by appealing to the moral conscience of America.

President Kennedy had been assassinated in 1963 (the same year professor Timothy Leary was fired by Harvard for involving students in experiments with a drug called LSD). But then came Lyndon B. Johnson, promising a Great Society, and it boggles one's memory to recall that even the SDS people were marginal supporters of Johnson as late as the November elections of 1964. Their slogan: "Part of the Way with LBJ."

It also is instructive to re-examine past issues of *Time* magazine. The journal's Man of the Year in 1967 was the Now Generation (people 25 and under) and the young man on the cover is a cleancut youth with short hair who is wearing a necktie. In its cover story, *Time* noted that the Man of the Year appeared to be "increasingly perturbed by the war." But the photographic emphasis was still on the annual beer bust at Fort Lauderdale in Florida, as opposed to the police bust on the barricades, and *Time* informed its readers: "At a majority of colleges and universities, there have been no student demonstrations against anything." *Time* added: " . . . today's youth appears more deeply committed to the fundamental Western ethos—decency, tolerance, brotherhood—than any generation since the age of chivalry. If they have an ideology, it is idealism."

Implied in that idealism was a simple faith in the good will of the American people: a naive assumption that it was necessary only to present the people with the facts, and they would rise up to end injustice; that passionate preaching could dissolve evil structures and expose wicked men. As a fellow radical recalls telling the SDS's Tom Hayden at the time: "Tom, you're so grassroots I don't know whether I should follow you or water you."

The slow erosion of student idealism might be traced back to the 1964 Democratic National Convention and the abortive attempt to seat the Mississippi Freedom Delegation. Then came 1965 and the escalation of our commitment in Vietnam. But even in that year only 7 per cent of America's college students favored immediate withdrawal from Vietnam, and as late as 1967 almost half the students still classified themselves as hawks.

The explosion occurred in 1968.

Look at the *Time* issue of June 7, 1968. On its cover is a young man representing the 1968 college graduate. Under his mortarboard he wears long hair, a beard, and a surly expression. And the cover story expresses editorial alarm over the emergence of a "relatively small group of radicals who hate all authority." Worse yet, they also hated capitalism.

A new dimension had been added to the nature of student protest in the spring of 1968, when students occupied five buildings at Columbia University in New York City. This reflected not only a change in tactics but also a change in objectives. American universities were now under attack as agents of the war machine, because of their cooperation in military research; as agents of racism, because of their corporate policies; as agents of political repression, because their educational mills were supplying the social managers who ran the nation's technetronic power structure. The new idea was to seize the universities and turn them into an alternative power base—into a political weapon that could be used to change the structure of the larger society. This in turn reflected a direct assault upon the institutions of that society; an assault upon "the system."

The system, of course, was capitalism, and the assault upon it meant that the SDS at least had abandoned all hope of idealistic reformism. The vast majority of activist students had not yet done so, as they demonstrated that summer by their "Clean for Gene" campaign efforts during the presidential primaries. But even their idealism could not survive the year.

It was a very bad year.

Dr. Martin Luther King Jr., the continuous symbol, was murdered in

April. Robert F. Kennedy, ghost of the late President, was murdered in June. Hubert H. Humphrey was nominated in August, after the Chicago convention riots, and Richard M. Nixon was elected in November. And in that same interval there also perished the politics of idealism.

The SDS died the following summer, when it split hopelessly asunder on factional lines during its 1969 convention in Chicago. The Progressive Labor faction went off to organize the working class, and the Weatherman faction went underground to build bombs—after expressing its frustrations in the Days of Rage rioting in Chicago that October. As a critic of radical persuasion put it, the typical PL organizer wouldn't know a worker if one bit him in the leg. And the bombmakers were mainly successful in blowing up themselves.

Campus disruptions continued in 1969, including Columbia-style occupation of buildings by students at Harvard and the University of Chicago, and across the country there were literally thousands of bombings, attempted bombings and bomb threats in 1969 and 1970.

The fact remains that campuses in 1969 were rapidly cooling. While the disruptive episodes that did occur tended to be more violent and dramatic than before, the number of such episodes was actually declining, and the violence itself can now be interpreted as evidence the radical Movement had reached a terminal stage. The trend would have been detected much earlier than it was, had it not been for the false impression created in the spring of 1970 by the widespread campus strikes following the Cambodian invasion and the student deaths at Kent State University and Jackson State College.

The President's Commission on Campus Unrest assessed the strikes as a radical victory, and the commission in fact reported that the radicals had succeeded in politicizing the nation's universities. Talk to students who participated in the 1970 affair, however, and most of them will recall it as more of a spring carnival than a political rebellion.

"That was the party week," said a philosophy senior at the University of Chicago. "And also the last gasp, I suppose. It was more or less expected of us, of course, and most of it was just keeping up with the Joneses. Other schools were on strike, and we had to preserve our radical reputation."

The best hindsight evidence for the political insignificance of the Cambodian spring was the Cambodian autumn. Coinciding with the release of the report by the unrest commission, Yale's President Kingman Brewster assessed the mood on campus with the opening of the fall term in 1970. And the mood he detected was one of "eerie tranquillity."

There was indeed a spooky interval on campus, and it lasted until the fall term in 1971. Its symptoms were apathy, pessimism, alienation, introversion, and increased involvement in drugs. As a Harvard don expressed it: "It wasn't the eerie tranquillity of a guerrilla fighter stalking in the jungle, ready to pounce again. It was exhaustion."

It can be said, then, that the events of 1968 represented not only the end of the beginning of a pseudo-revolutionary attack on American political institutions; they also marked the beginning of the end, if not indeed the end itself. After 1968, a small cadre of militants turned to terrorism. While they also rejected the politics of idealism, however, a majority of the former activist young people turned elsewhere.

They turned to Woodstock, and the short-lived phenomenon that was later described as the counterculture.

To understand this development, a brief flashback is required. The counterculture in fact had its roots in events that occurred prior to 1968, when youth protest split into two camps: the hippies and the heretics.

The heretics were the rather somber New Left activitists who believed it was the business of radicalism to change the structure of society by political action. They still basically accepted the materialistic orientation of the Old Left, discussing social justice in terms of income distribution and control of the production system. And you could not tell they were radicals unless they told you so; they wore short hair and neckties, and they didn't drop acid.

The hippies represented the alienated drug culture that had emerged on the West Coast around the middle of the decade. They had decided it was impossible to change the structure of society politically. The hippie solution was to drop out of society and change your own head—to change consciousness—through the use of psychedelic drugs. If you could not change reality, whatever that was, you could change your perception of reality. And reality perhaps was in the eye of the beholder. This, of course, was personal rather than social salvation; but hippies were optimistic that individual consciousness bending would ultimately result in social change as well, after drugs had turned on everybody in America to Ultimate Reality.

Hippies and heretics didn't like each other, and as late as 1967 it was still possible to tell one from the other. Heretics regarded hippies as irresponsible cop-outs, and hippies regarded heretics as materialistic Babbitts who shared the essential hangups of Middle America. But the two camps met in Chicago, at the 1968 Democratic National Convention. A third group called the Yippies also surfaced there, urging a youth coalition—suggesting that hippies should become more political and that heretics for their part should show more interest in life style.

The Movement after 1968 appeared to drift toward the proposed coalition, but it was the hippie element that actually prevailed. This, in turn, reflected a fundamental change in the nature of protest.

The emphasis now was on life style—including increased drug use, sexual permissiveness, communal herding, and a celebration of intuition and immediate experience. And the target of protest was not so much the system of production but technology itself; not the distribution of income but obsession with economic goods.

The gurus of this philosophy were Henry David Thoreau and Herbert

Marcuse. Thoreau had advocated voluntary poverty, charging that men had become the tools of their tools, and Marcuse taught that the machine in fact had become a political weapon, creating a one-dimensional society in which we produce more to consume more so we can produce more. Capital and labor collude to preserve the status quo, and it is no longer possible for most people even to conceive of alternative life styles in which they could enjoy the only real freedom; namely, "freedom from the economy." This thinking blended nicely with the emerging environmental issue. Our technology was killing us, and the only way to save ourselves was to scale down our technology and reduce our production. People must learn to ask a new question. Not: "How do I increase my income?" Rather: "How can I cut my needs?"

The result was the counterculture—consecrated by the Woodstock rock festival in August of 1969—which advocated the creation of an alternative culture that would challenge the Protestant work ethic by asserting that "more is less." As one of the new people put it, the idea was no longer to storm the castle; the idea was to stand outside the castle and make funny faces at the people inside.

What this actually represented was a return to the basic philosophy of the original hippies, which Charles A. Reich romanticized in his 1970 book *The Greening of America*. The central concept was that "consciousness precedes structure." Or as the Yippie court jester Abbie Hoffman expressed it: "Revolution is in my head. I am the Revolution."

It is doubtful there was anything in Abbie Hoffman's head. And the Revolution failed.

2

Paul is an aging radical even though he is barely cresting thirty. He was an early member of the S.D.S. and still wears a Castro-style beard and working-man's denims, which show his earlier affiliations. He stands before a group of people who have asked him to explain why he became a radical activist.

Paul:

I was brought up a Catholic and confession is very much a part of my life. After I got involved in the movement for social change in America, I got in the habit of making a public confession. I was very lucky. I got good grades and got a scholarship to Harvard and I spent several years as a graduate student. I was looking for people, for models to imitate. I thought that I might have wanted to be a professor at Harvard.

I used to pick up the New York Times *and read about the escalation of the war in Vietnam and I'd read about the rebellions in the black ghettos and I somehow felt that something was happening in the world and I didn't know what it was. The biggest thing was the civil rights movement. When I was a kid graduated from college, I was opposed to it. I thought it was Communist inspired.*

At one point, I had a decision to make. I was offered a scholarship from Harvard to finish my dissertation in Europe. But I also had a choice to teach as a Woodrow Wilson intern in a black school in the South and I decided to interrupt my promising career for one year. Just take one year out of my life and give it to the good causes. It didn't happen that way because when I came back from the South a year later, I was a different person. I learned a lot. I thought I went down there with things to teach people but it turns out I had so much to learn.

From then on my life was never going to be the same. I got into the Movement deeper and deeper and joined the S.D.S. eventually. I want to be together with other people engaged not just in living, not just getting a paycheck every two weeks and raising a family. I want to do all that, I want to raise a family but I don't want to raise them in this world, not in this world I see around me. I want them to grow up in a different world because sometimes I feel despaired. I don't see much evidence . . .

Tony: *Why such militancy?*

Paul: *Well it seems to me, although formally we have a democratic system, our problem is that the formal institutions like the ballot box just don't operate very well. Our institutions are controlled by a tiny elite and I'm referring to the large corporations and the giant bureaucracy—that these are controlled by a relatively small number of rich people. The executives of US Steel together with a few bankers can decide or make decisions about production that will affect the lives of thousands of people.*

Tony: *O.K., Paul, let's say that I agree with you, but let's say we take all the officials out of US Steel today and we put in all new people. Ultimately what would happen is someone has to make all the decisions . . .*

Paul: *. . . and the question is to whom they are handed . . .*

Tony: *Have you ever been with a group of people, I mean look at how many diverse opinions there are here and I am sure we would all have a different opinion on what procedure or what path we should take with the corporation.*

Paul: *That's precisely why we have to solve it by a democratic process. The people who now make our decisions are not a diverse group.*

Tony: *O.K. Take all these people out. Who do we put in there? How is anything going to be any different? Don't you think that the same thing could be taking place, that there would be a certain few in power?*

Paul: *That's the problem that any movement or any people's government has to face and that can be resolved only by more democracy, not by being afraid of it. That can only be resolved by the collective strength of the organized people.*

Tony: *Yeah, but . . .*

Paul: *And it won't work perfectly.*

Tony: *Why go to such extremes to get what you want? Are we going to need that much change? Paul, you are fighting the system and this is your way of fighting. You thought you could beat it this way?*

Paul: *Yeah. I thought I could pull it off. I could fight it and at the same time be respected, loved and embraced by it.*

Tony: *You're still like a martyr.*

Paul: *Well, I guess there is evidence of that. I don't really agree that the struggle always comes first. I can't sacrifice my family. I guess to some extent I'm using the system. I know that if I can't get a job for whatever reason we'll get enough money to shelter ourselves, and that probably wouldn't be true in many societies in which I'd oppose the system. So I'm still relying on the decency and institutional relationships of this society and I still don't think this is an entirely rotten society. Perhaps as good as other human societies have ever been. Partly when I appear to be attacking it, I'm not attacking it because I hate it but because I love it. I am a part of it and I would like some of the things it says come true.*

2.
Death of the Movement

Mammy Yokum, the celebrated philosopher, once observed that good is better than evil because it's nicer. In the same spirit, the President's Commission on Campus Unrest declared: "Violence must stop because it is wrong." The commission also reported that student rebellion had reached crisis proportions; that the divisions in American society paralleled those of the Civil War; that the level of violence was steadily rising; that a continuation of present trends would threaten "the very survival of the nation."

The commission's report was submitted September 26, 1970.

As noted in the previous chapter, the crisis by then had already passed. It had lasted in fact only a few years and reached its flash point in 1968. After that there was a fundamental change in the character of youthful protest that ultimately resulted in the dropping of the torch, in the death of the radical Movement.

This chapter will attempt an autopsy. We will ask why the politics of idealism in the 1960s degenerated into a politics of confrontation, a politics of revolutionary terrorism, and finally an apolitical counterculture.

Looking first at the question of violence, it seems clear at this point that idealism is not a very substantial foundation on which to base a successful political movement; that the progression to terrorism—from preaching to bombing—was an almost inevitable dialectic. Reflecting on this idea, Martin Peretz commented:

"I once said that when Hubert Humphrey talks you know everything is desperate, but you're not clear what's important. And I had the same sense about the students—that they were terribly intense and passionate, but I don't know how serious. I mean, you'd hear students say they were radicals. And I would suppose a radical analysis of America would be a very tough-minded analysis which would recognize that the problems of this society, and its policies, have very deep roots. But I would have people say to me: 'Look, we've done everything. We went to New Hampshire. We marched.' And since all that failed, the next step was that much more justifiable.

"Well, it is not a radical analysis to think that because there were marches in the country that maybe brought out 700,000 people—or two million even— that the fundamental tendencies of American society were going to be reversed. That's what I mean by 'serious'. People said to me: 'We're tired of losing.' Therefore you assume another more militant tactic which is even more certain to lose. And it's very much in the American mode to think that if one strategy doesn't work in three months, you move on to another. But the effort to change this society will take a very long time. And it can not succeed simply by dramatic moral assertion."

A comparable theory was offered by Michael Harrington.

"I'd give a sort of standard Marxist analysis," he said. "I think the terrorism is the result of a philosophy that substitutes individuals for a mass movement. In other words, terrorism is essentially a confession of failure. And it starts with the concept of a substitute proletariat.

"Marx of course assigned the working class the role of being the historic agency for the transformation of society and the making of the revolution. And the history of the New Left in the 1960s is in considerable measure a history of searching for a new proletariat, or what I've referred to as the substitute proletariat. The first substitute was the student himself, and that goes back to the Port Huron manifesto when the SDS was founded. But it turned out that didn't work quite so well. So then it became the black man. But the black man didn't play the role he was supposed to play, quite. So then it became the poor. But the poor refused to play the role, too. So that was one factor, the disappointment in the substitute proletariat. Another thing is that the war deepened the alienation of these kids from society, and the more desperate of them tried to substitute themselves for the proletariat. That is to say, a handful of people armed with bombs became the new proletariat. And I think that was terrible. I think it was elitist. I think it was self-satisfied, super-theoretical, upper-middle-class elitism in the form of proletarian radicalism. I think it had nothing to do with the working class or oppressed minorities as they actually are."

One of the blacks who refused to play the requested role for the white radicals is Eva Scott, a community leader in Washington, D. C. Confronting an audience of shabbily-dressed students at the University of Colorado, she said: "It makes me sick to look at you. I see poor black kids wearing $65 dollar shoes, and I know why they do that. Because they really experience poverty. And you white kids in your old clothes are playing games with me. You're free not to be poor."

The President's commission proposed there are built-in, evolutionary forces that tend to move protest behavior to extremism: "To the extent that audience reaction was the proximate goal of student protest, the activists were at any given moment under a strong incentive to express themselves a little louder and a bit more forcefully than the last time—otherwise there was a possibility that people would become accustomed to acts of protest and begin to ignore them. Thus, the simple passing of time spurred the movement to go farther and farther afield of the tactics and perspectives of instrumentalist, reformist politics, and closer and closer to a thoroughgoing radical strategy."

If that passage implies that violence is inherent in the momentum of radical politics, it should be pointed out from an historical perspective that most violence in this country has had a "conservative" bias. As the historian Richard Hofstadter has written: "It has been unleashed against abolitionists, Catholics, radicals, workers and labor organizers, Negroes, Orientals, and other ethnic or racial or ideological minorities, and has been used ostensibly to protect the American, the Southern, the white Protestant, or simply the established middle-class way of life and morals."

Also, it could be argued that the commission's analysis makes more sense in reverse; that it was in fact the lack of a coherent radical strategy that moved the students toward violence.

To touch on a tender point, political violence in some cases may have psychological origins. In the past, it was usually considered crude reductionism even to suggest that possibility. But there are pragmatic reasons to do so. If some dropped-out activists were into the Movement for therapy, as now seems likely, radicals perhaps should do a little reading in Freud as well as Marx— if only for the purpose of counting their horses, as Chicago politicians like to put it: to learn whom to trust for continued and prudent support.

One popular theory relates political tantrums to permissive childcare. If a kid was picked up every time he cried, and fed on demand, he would not learn to tolerate even moderate frustration. Or to put it in Freudian jargon: he would grow up with an inadequate ego structure, would be dominated by his id and the pleasure principle, and would reject the reality principle. This provides a psychoanalytic explanation of the "nonnegotiable demand." Such a person would also imagine that his wishes had a magic power to transform reality. If he wished for a revolution, he would feel certain the country was tottering on the very brink of revolution—no matter what the reality principle had to say on the subject.

A former SDS member at Harvard attributed that kind of thinking to the press, not his id. "You guys in the media gave us so much coverage, we thought revolution was right around the corner. You gave us an inflated idea of our own strength. And that's what killed the SDS, as a matter of fact. Thanks a lot." Another former SDS member, who has since turned Buddhist, attributed the notion of inflated strength to the FBI and the late J. Edgar Hoover. "He always looked at a far brighter side than I did."

Another psychiatric theory, more demonstrable than the first, has to do with the fact that everybody has some aggressive feelings. And there are basically only two ways to handle them. You can internalize them or externalize them, turn them in on yourself or outward on others. During the London blitz in World War II, psychiatric clinics in that city admitted almost no new patients, and the hypothesis was that Londoners were directing all their aggressions against the Nazi bombers. After the blitz, the clinics filled up again. Similarly, psychiatric directors at a number of universities reported that the number of students requesting treatment increased sharply after the peak period of campus turmoil.

"The external violence was never that great anyway," said Kevin Starr, a senior tutor at Harvard. "I mean, the worst student violence was chickenfeed compared to Attica. The really freaky stuff was the internal thing: rotting your head with acid, the patterns of self-destruction, the dropping out."

Cultural anthropologist Edward T. Hall offered a long-range view.

"America was basically unprepared for world leadership after World War II," he said, "and we took on tremendous responsibilities without the psychological and moral preparations we needed to do that. World War II and the depression were the last unifying experiences this country had, and we paid a heavy price, particularly during the war, with our children. Because two things happened.

"Prior to the war, we had a tremendous influx of immigrants. Their children grew up in the United States and rejected the culture of the parents—and, along with it, parental authority and stability. Then many of these children either went to war or went to work in war industries, and their children in turn were left to raise themselves. And this was done on a vast scale, and the result was a vast erosion of discipline following World War II.

"Then Joe McCarthy came along in 1950 and started destroying people for political expediency. And nobody came to their defense. Not even President Eisenhower. And when the President would not come to the rescue of the State Department and people he knew were completely innocent, this served notice on everybody that times had changed. It meant that bullies had an open season; they could take out after anybody they wanted to, and there was no protection against bullies.

"And then the next thing that happened was President Kennedy's destruction by a rather normal paranoid individual of which there are, if not millions, hundreds of thousands in this country. Adlai Stevenson was spat upon in Dallas just before this happened, and he warned the President. He said: "You must not go there. That town is crazy. There is something happening there.' And Mr. Kennedy was not on to these things. But there was something happening there. And the assassination turned loose another dreadful outpouring of hate in the United States. The message was that any public figure was now fair game, just for nuts or anybody. If you don't like the way he does things, shoot him.

"Most people of course were shocked and distressed. But if you're somebody who's a little close to the edge, or if you think people have been picking on you, and life has treated you badly, and then somebody who's just like you goes out and shoots a President—well, oh boy. We'd have violence before, but until that time it had been to some extent controlled. But this unleashed an uncontrolled type of violence—the whole thing with the kids, the hijacking of planes. Everybody thought he could do whatever he goddamn well pleased. How does that song go? 'If it feels good, do it.' Hijack a plane. Shoot the President. Destroy the State Department. Whatever it was, you could get away with it.

"There used to be authority figures who said: 'Look, buster, beyond this you don't go.' And this was the President who did not call a halt to McCarthy. And it was the President who got shot. So this meant literally, it wasn't God who was dead—but Father was dead. And Father not only hadn't kept control over younger brother—kept a leash on him, which he should have done—but now younger brother had killed Father."

The pattern of violence was altered by three events in 1970: the fatal shooting of six students at Kent State University and Jackson State College, and the explosion of a terrorist bomb which killed a student researcher and injured four persons at the University of Wisconsin at Madison.

The shootings demonstrated that violent protest could end in death, and students were shocked by them. But the real impact was felt that summer, when students across the country went home and heard their own parents tell them: "They should have shot more. If you had been there, they should have shot you." For the first time perhaps, students recognized the degree of adult hostility that existed against them—hostility that had shot above the boiling point during the Cambodian strikes. If nothing else, the national response convinced many radicals America was not ripe for a mass-movement Revolution.

But the Madison bombing probably had even greater impact, summed up in the reaction of an Iowa Wesleyan College freshman who was a high school radical at the time. He remembers the first thought that flashed through his mind when he heard the news from Madison: "Holy Moses. I'm completely wrong."

"All that rhetoric," said a Harvard junior. "Like 'off the pigs.' I thought it was just talk. When I found out what violence really was, it scared the hell out of me."

His remark reflects the fact that most student activists came from liberal middle-class homes, where physical violence is not taught as a value. Disputes in such homes, ideally, are supposed to be settled by democratic discussion. Conflict and hostility are expressed verbally, with words instead of punches. Now students discovered words could lead to mangled bodies; they also discovered they had Cain in them as well as Abel. They learned the meaning of Marianne Moore's line: "I must fight till I have conquered in myself what causes war." And the effect was profound. While it did not change their social values, Madison did cause many activists to reconsider their idealistic image of themselves and the morality of their tactics.

If Kent State and Jackson State were the Hiroshima and Nagasaki of the Movement, Madison was its My Lai. But factors other than violence also were responsible for the collapse of the Movement, and one of those factors was Little Brother.

Beware of Little Brother. Little Brother is watching you. Little Brother is going to make a Revolution.

Remember him?

He's the kid that militant college students used to warn you about in the late 1960s. "You think I'm radical? Wait'll you see my little brother who's in high school right now. He's really a radical. When he gets on campus, he's going to blow this place to hell."

The kid's on campus now, and he appears in many cases to be under deep sedation. If you ask him why he is not engaged in radical activity, he will tell you: "Oh, that. I did all that in high school."

The educator Nathan Pusey once said the biggest mistake the SDS ever made was its effort to organize the high schools. While the SDS wasn't really responsible, high school students did become politicized during the same period (after 1968) that universities were starting to become depoliticized. By the time they entered college, most of the students had exhausted their political energies.

The same point was made, unintentionally, by a former SDS organizer in Chicago who describes himself as "actively unactive." He said: "It's a funny thing. The above-ground Movement that used to be the New Left is getting younger and younger. In fact it seemed to me that a lot of people who were Weatherman advocates were of high school age, and when I was working with SDS in 1967 and 1968 we were just beginning to talk about organizing the high schools with an education program. We were behind the times, obviously, because the high schools were already revolting on their own. And today, the active age level for a revolutionary seems to be around 14 or 15. Go to any activist hangout, like Alice's, and they can hardly reach the bar."

To the extent that radicalism was a fad, it followed the evolutionary path of most other campus-bred fads. Proms, for example. And drugs. (One reason drug abuse is no longer an acute problem at the college level is that little brother also did all that in high school.) But the almost neurotic intensity of protest activity in the 1960s could not have sustained itself in any case, even if high schools had not been politicized.

After the surface calm of the 1950s, young people in the 1960s had their circuits overloaded with promises of a New Frontier and a Great Society. But the Kennedy-Johnson monuments, as opposed to their rhetoric, were Cuba, bomb shelters, Vietnam, and a racially-polarized society. As young people gradually became aware of this, their fuses blew. After 1968, as we have seen, a minority of activists expressed their disillusionment in a spurt of terrorism; a majority sank into a mood of existential despair and alienation that lasted until the start of the 1971-72 academic year, when students appeared to have recovered their psychological balance—concentrating on their studies and the rational management of their private lives.

At the time, this was attributed in large part to the recession. And it is clear now that economic affluence was indeed a major factor in initiating the decade of youthful activism. Consider the testimony of Michael Wadleigh, the young film-maker who won an Oscar for his movie *Woodstock*. Looking back on the early days of that decade, he said:

"There was so much money around. And therefore the middle-class students had leisure. Then the blacks got education—at least a few of them—and those who got educated started looking around and said: 'Hey, baby, you know, I mean what the hell, I might as well try to lead my people out of this.' I think it was as simple as that, as far as the black thing went. But do you know how I went down South, in a very real way? What brought me down to Mississippi —and I went down more than once, and very early, in high school—what took me down there was a goddamn Chevrolet that I owned. Because I could get an easy job and work a few hours and buy a goddamn car when I was 16. My father didn't even have to give it to me. I went to Mississippi because I had the car, and free summers, and it was a hell of a lot more exciting thing to do than to drive again to New York or Florida. And then slowly but surely I got caught up in it. Predictably enough, you turn very idealistic; when you have enough money you can afford to be extremely idealistic."

For a generation without even Jungian memories of the depression, the economic pressures generated by the recession probably relieved some of the psychological pressures of extended adolescence—the mental distress that sometimes afflicts fully-pubertal young people confined in ivy-covered deten-tion camps. With tuition, scholarships, and the job market to worry about, students had little time to brood over social injustice and metaphysical abstractions.

Another psychological pressure was removed by the failure of the Move-ment.

The Movement at its zenith had never attracted more than a small per-centage of students who were seriously committed to radical activism; it now seems apparent that a substantial number of students were only marginal militants, and that many of these were motivated by peer pressure. A group of graduate students at the Yale Drama School were talking about this over a pitcher of beer, and one of them said: "I remember this really fantastic pres-sure to be political. And a lot of it, to be effective, called for a really full-time commitment. I joined a couple demonstrations, which was easy to do. But to be really effective was almost a full-time job, and I wasn't ready for that. Do your best in one thing, I always thought. So I've been concentrating on my work here, on my studies."

A bearded, sad-eyed youth sitting next to him said: "I've never been in-terested in politics. I'm older—29—and I only went to one demonstration, after Kent State. Otherwise I always felt it was like a fad that rode on the coat tails of other things, like drugs and the genuine thing with the black kids. White radicals had always been around, and I always felt sorry for them; I always felt like they had a real poverty of the imagination, getting pumped up over things that weren't real. But one thing gave me a great deal of trouble. A political person would say: 'If you're not a part of the solution, you're a part of the problem.' And I'd lie awake thinking about that, because it seemed irrefutable. And yet . . . it was just that I knew all the time there was nothing I could really do."

"Did the person ever say what the solution was?" he was asked.

"No, as a matter of fact. And now that I think of it, I'm glad you said that. I'm sick of people telling me that other crap."

"Thank God it's over," said a philosophy senior at the University of Chicago. "Those mass meetings especially. They used to have mass meetings here constantly. And I don't know if you ever had the unfortunate experience of going to one, but they were long-winded, dull, stupid. They were mostly procedural debates, and they'd go on for ten hours sometimes, and nobody ever convinced anybody of anything."

"What strikes me is that there's been so little change," said sociologist Andrew M. Greeley. "I mean, the fashion has changed. Where the fashion arbiters on campus are is not where they used to be. But the amazing thing is that the football stadiums were not empty in 1968 or 1969. People went to football games then. People took exams, people were studying for professional careers, people fell in love and got married. And that continues. So there's a sort of glacial-like similarity to all semesters, and the differences have to do with maybe 5 per cent of the college population and say another 15 or 20 per cent that's deeply influenced by this 5 per cent. That is to say, you probably never had more than 20 to 25 percent of the college population that was even somewhat involved in the radical thing, and only about 5 percent of that was deeply involved.

"Well, that 5 percent has changed. And since that 5 percent is what sets the tone on campus, of course the tone has changed. But the striking thing to me is the continuity. We had radical groups in the past. And we had a radical period recently. And now that's apparently over. I think the mistake a lot of people made was to identify a passing campus phenomenon with a permanent trend. I think you could probably make a case that there is a long-run trend for social concern, dating all the way back to the Peace Corps. But how that social concern is going to be manifested is not at this point obvious. The volunteer movement has failed, the radical movement has failed. What's left? For some kids the only thing that seems to be left is dropping out, in the full sense of the term; withdrawing from society and moving off to some sort of permanent gypsy life.

"But again, this is only going to be a minority. And the fact is, a lot of us have made the mistake of judging a book by its cover; to think because a kid looks like a drug addict, he is. Because the vast majority of college kids are not hippies. They are not radicals. They are not anything. They may wear their hair long. They may wear hippie clothes and listen to rock music and may even smoke pot. But they're as square as their parents. And the truth of the matter is, the student generation is square. And you can quote me. These kids are not politically sophisticated; they don't know beans about politics. They're not politically committed. They're dull, middle-class clods."

A statistical perspective was added by political analyst Sidney Hyman, who said:

"When you look at the actual number of conflict campuses—the actual number that were distressed during the 1960s by violence—there were not more than 120. You had 2,000 campuses that were so calm you'd have thought they were cemeteries. The student activist who was at the forefront of all this imagined the whole world was ripe for revolution because he was, or thought he was. The police chief who was trying to put down this riot thought everybody had gone off his rocker. So it went. From one group to another, this was the illusion. And everybody started to generalize.

"The realities were different. And let me give you one reality. The SDS, at the maximum height of its power, never had more than 7,000 dues-paying members, out of a student population of more than seven million, with a possible 35,000 who were supporters but not dues-paying members. Well,

I'm sure you could fill Madison Square Garden with 35,000 people in this country who believe in cannibalism. But that still leaves you with more than two hundred million who don't."

The failure of the counterculture will be discussed later. The counterculture did raise important questions about the future of the work ethic, to be examined in the last chapter, but it was obviously premature in a scarcity economy. Politically, it was about as subversive as baseball—easily co-opted and an excellent market for capitalist enterprise—and it has been referred to indeed as the over-the-counterculture. It has sold millions of dollars in phonograph records, and it created in pornography a new major industry. *The Whole Earth Catalog,* its first secret scripture, has now won the National Book Award.

If most young people today are preoccupied with their educations and personal lives, that is only natural and even healthy. The feverish student activism of the 1960s was abnormal to the extent that it was based on a conviction Revolution was imminent in America. Studies and personal concerns often were neglected in an almost wartime atmosphere. And it would be unrealistic in the present situation to expect a majority of young people to commit themselves to the militant-activist role.

The campus after all is a microcosm of the larger society, which has to go about its business. There have always been dedicated activists in the society, and they have always been relatively few in number. "When we organized the packinghouse workers in Chicago," said Saul Alinsky, "we had maybe seventy people who were really active. When we organized Back of the Yards we had about 5 percent active participation, which I didn't realize then was a tremendous amount."

There will still be demonstrations in America, as long as the war in Vietnam continues, and campuses might well erupt temporarily in response to some unmitigated outrage. But opposition to the war is hardly radical activity— Republican grandmothers are against the war—and the overwhelming majority of students have no interest whatever in working for a political Revolution.

Most students, however, retain a commitment to advanced social policy— a commitment that might be expressed in the simple act of voting. And those who remain active may well be more effective in the future, now that they have stopped thinking in terms of apocalyptic quantum leaps to a Green (or Red) America. They are in a self-critical frame of mind, asking where they screwed up, and they have accepted the fact that successful political struggles take generations. They might be compared with those early Christians who had expected the second coming to occur in the immediate future, ushering in the Kingdom of God. Convinced now they may have a long wait, they are in the process of forming a visible church of radicalism.

Meanwhile, what about those young people from a few years back who really bought the whole thing: dropping acid, dropping out, going underground to await the Revolution? Many of them are degenerating in the cities, doing nothing at all or working as street cleaners. "Take a taxi at Harvard Square," said a professor, "and chances are one in four the driver will be a 1969 summa cum laude from Cornell."

A significant number of these people have been returning to school, working furiously to make up for those wasted years, and this has been described as the drop-in phenomenon. Of the others, it can truly be said that they represent a lost generation. And an American tragedy.

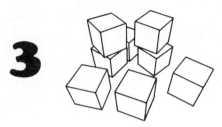

3

A family convenes on a television stage. The mother stands to introduce her youngest daughter and describes some hopes she has for the girl. Mother and daughter talk while grandmother listens quietly, as long as she can.

Mary: **(Mother)**	*This is my daughter, Jeannie. She's 15, she's going to be 16 soon. She's my second daughter. Kathleen is the oldest. In all sincerity, I should say I want Jeannie to be a good person, according to her definition of good. That's first and foremost. But then I find myself in a very ambivalent position, too. I find myself talking like parents sometimes in a way that I never thought I would. I want Jeannie to make the most of her potential. So, I'd like her to help change the world, make it a little better place to be happy. But, I also want her to expand her potentials so that she's the fullest kind of person that she can be.*
Jeannie: **(Daughter)**	*I know what I want to be. I know what I want to do and most of it is what you want me to be also. I want to have a lot of contact with people.*
Dorothy: **(Grand- mother)**	*Why don't you just lay down a few rules for this girl. If you want so much for her, don't you think you should take care of the responsibility?*
Mary:	*What do you mean take my responsibility?*
Dorothy:	*Well, you're giving her too much freedom. Do you think at 15 she knows what she wants? Do you think you should give her a little more guidance?*
Mary:	*I give her guidance but I can't . . .*
Dorothy:	*Did we let you do what you wanted at age 15?*
Mary:	*No.*
Dorothy:	*Mary, you know you talk too much. Why do you do so much*

Mary: *talking with your kids? You know it doesn't do any good.*
                                I think this is marvelous. I mean I'm glad she's talking to me.

Now the father and an older daughter take over. Their talk is more serious because they uncover some difficulties that underlie exchanges between parents and children.

Kathy: *Wait a minute, Daddy. The reason I did not go through high school a year early is because Mommy didn't approve of it and she told me that. She says that she's trying to let me make my own decisions. She won't force me to her opinion but it's there and . . .*

Ray: *Well, we can't hide our own personal feelings from you but we certainly try to give you as much freedom as possible.*

Kathy: *I know, but I thought perhaps she was right and for that reason I did not advance.*

Ray: *O.K. Fine.*

Kathy: *You know, I'm in a lot more control of myself than I was two years ago.*

Ray: *I hope so. Two years from now, you'll be in much better control.*

Kathy: *Yes, that's exactly why I want to wait a year before I go to college. Two years ago you viewed my opinions as not well thought out and just irrational, but you really haven't talked to me in a long time. You haven't really noticed how I've developed emotionally. I don't think you really know how objective I can be.*

Ray: *We're talking right now, aren't we?*

Kathy: *Yes. But you are letting your impression of me blind this conversation. You do not expect the things I say to be serious. You are thinking to yourself: 'This is my daughter. She's only 16. She's irrational. She grows two years at a time.'*

Ray: *Well, why don't you put yourself in my place, Kathy? It's very difficult being a parent. This is the first time I've had to face this problem. I've thought it over previously and run it through but it's hitting home right now. I don't think it's a good thing that you're doing. You must realize that letting go is very difficult for a parent . . . from the time a child is born to let her go.*

3.
Inventing the Kids

We used to call them college men, and college women. Now they're college kids.

The change occurred during the 1960s—the decade of youth protest—and it crept into the language almost unconsciously, reflecting what appeared to be a weird and profound transformation in the relationship between the generations. It was during the 1960s that the news media reported the emergence of a generation gap, and it became fashionable for young people to have what was referred to as an identity crisis. The young were said to be alienated, from their parents and from adult society in general.

But there is evidence now that the generation gap has closed, if it ever really existed, and most young people recently have been too busy to spend much time wondering who they are. "To hell with it," said a Harvard student, forking health foods into his mouth during lunch in Eliot House. "I'm alienated with being alienated. And so are a lot of people I know." "Carlyle said it's impossible to know yourself," said a philosophy major at the university of Chicago. "He said to know what you can work at. And that's what I'm trying to do now."

Historically, the adolescent is a comparatively recent invention of industrial society. Until a few hundred years ago in fact there was no such thing even as childhood. Children did not exist. There were just little people and big people. In medieval art, for example, children were painted as tiny adults, wearing adult clothing and adult expressions. Infant mortality was so high that parents paid little attention to young people until they reached the age of seven or so, at which point they were admitted at once into adulthood.

The big people and little people worked and played together. Boys went to brothels and taverns, where they gambled at cards and dice. Parents rolled hoops and joined their offspring in snowball fights. And the little people did not go to school; they worked as household servants or as apprentices to craftsmen and artists. According to the cultural historian Philippe Ariès, the concept of childhood as a stage of life didn't fully develop until the seventeenth century—when Christian moralists decided the little people needed more time to grow up, and protected education. So children and schools were invented at the same time, and children were people who went to school.

In the early industrial period, most children left school early to work in the factories and mills. And as soon as they did, they were treated as little adults. It was only in the modern era that increased affluence allowed a third stage of life called adolescence.

Adolescence should not be confused with puberty, which is a period of biological change. Adolescence corresponded with an extension of education, and adolescents were people who went to high school. Until the last decade, people who went to college were generally considered an intellectual elite of pre-professionals and were thought of as young adults: as college men, and college women.

Adolescence was also described, by the analyst Erik H. Erikson, as a psychosocial moratorium: as a period of grace in which young people are given time to define themselves psychologically and to decide upon their ultimate social role, to figure out who they are and what they want to do as adults. And it is during the moratorium, faced with so many choices and so many decisions to make, that young people are supposed to experience the mental storm and stress of the identity crisis.

In the 1960s, as we saw in the first chapter, the postwar baby boom, parental affluence, and the Sputnik scare jammed colleges and universities with millions of young people—many of whom, in earlier days, would probably have gone directly from high school into the labor market and psychosocial adulthood.

Many of these young people did not really want to go to college. Many of them did not really need more education to prepare for their careers. And the massive enrollments in themselves contributed to a deterioration in the quality of college life, turning many institutions into impersonal multiversities. These institutions also, in many cases, were now closely associated with government and industry (the military-industrial-educational complex), emphasizing research and the training of highly-specialized social managers, as opposed to traditional concepts of undergraduate education.

The new students frequently remained financially dependent upon their parents. Their educations were subsidized; they had free summers and an abundance of leisure during the academic year, and many of them prolonged the moratorium by delaying a decision on their choice of a career. There developed in consequence a campus-based subculture of young people who found sodality in music and drugs and social activism.

Clearly there was something different about this college generation. They seemed too old and sophisticated to be described as adolescents. And yet, they also seemed too restless and confused to be described even as young adults. Observing them—and extrapolating from Erikson's psychosocial concept— the Yale psychologist Kenneth Keniston suggested that they represented the development in America of a new, fourth stage of life.

Keniston proposed that these young people were *psychological adults*—in the sense that they had established an inner identity, had demonstrated intellectual competence, had come to terms with their sexuality, and could relate meaningfully to other people. But they were *sociological adolescents*—in the sense that they remained disengaged from society, did not have jobs, and had not committed themselves to a lasting relationship with one sex partner.

Keniston called this new stage of life "youth" (the new sequence now being childhood-adolescence-youth-adulthood). He said it might last almost a decade, spanning perhaps the ages 18 to 26, and he added, "Upper-middle-class families in particular do not consider it alarming for their children to remain unemployed and unmarried until the age of 30—as long as they are in school."

I asked Erikson if he agreed with Keniston's extrapolation, and Erikson said: "No. I don't think you can in fact separate the sociological and the psychological. Since my concept is psychosocial, obviously you can't separate the two."

But many people found the youth theory attractive, and indeed the idea developed that the moratorium might be extended to infinity: that it might become a permanent way of life. The result was the short-lived counterculture that emerged after 1968.

The counterculture collapse, due in part to the recession and in part to unresolved psychological pressures. While it may have been an omen of the future, it was premature in a scarcity economy and a society in which identity is still closely associated with a person's social function or occupational role. While it lasted, however, it contributed to the popular impression of a significant gap.

But even at the time, research data indicated the gap was superficial and largely a myth. In 1963, for example, psychiatrist Daniel Offer began a long-range study of middle-class boys entering high school in two affluent Chicago suburbs (Evanston and Park Forest, the latter the home town of William H.

Whyte's organization man). Offer followed them all the way through high school, conducting frequent interviews, and reported his findings after they had graduated. He found that these young people for the most part shared their parents' middle-class values and seldom rebelled against parental authority—except for minor bickering that occurred mostly during early adolescence. He concluded:

"The teen-agers we studied were by and large an integral part of the culture within which they lived. They were proud of their schools, their communities, and the achievements of their parents. It is our impression that, for better or worse, the sample investigated by us is growing up to become very much a part of the culture into which they were born."

Most of the teen-agers went on to college, where Offer continued to study them, and they graduated in June of 1971 from thirty different institutions. Discussing the results of his project, Offer said:

"The values these students shared with their parents have remained intact. We rotated the most important variables through a computer, and the computer suggests the generation gap has been way overplayed. I don't believe it exists. Even among the radical young there's a sharing of values with the parents. The gap that exists is not between generations. It's a gap between different groups in the total population, young and old."

Offer was referring to the so-called red diaper theory: the idea that the radical students of the 1960s tended to come from liberal-to-radical homes and saw themselves essentially as extending the values of their parents. If any conflict existed, it was usually based upon the disappointing perception that the parents themselves had not lived up to their values; that the parents had copped out.

That theory is supported by firm data and suggests once again that the youth population is a microcosm of the larger adult society. As a University of Chicago philosophy student expressed it:

"I know I look very counterculturish, with my beard and all. But I think if you talked to me long you'd find me quite dull and unexceptional. And I'm pretty typical, really. You're not dealing, I think, with a significantly different generation—in the sense of having completely different values. Students may behave somewhat differently than their parents, and dress differently, and different institutions are created. But you don't have people who think wildly different from their folks. You never did."

"I think most of the radical kids became more radical than their parents," said a student at Iowa Wesleyan College. "And they had this idea the parents had sold out to the establishment. But then, through their experiences in later years, they ended up with pretty much the same liberal values the parents had. I mean, they found out why the parents sold out. And that ends the generation gap, when that point in time comes."

Offer's studies also indicate that the celebrated identity crisis is not in fact experienced by a majority of young people.

"Everybody keeps telling you you're supposed to have one," said an 18-year-old English major at Iowa Wesleyan. "Like you wake up feeling fine, and everybody tells you all day you look sick. But I've never had one yet, as far as I can tell. Sometimes it worries me."

A friend of his commented:

"I thought I had a very serious identity crisis a few years ago, as a result of suddenly-increased freedom. You're living at home with your parents, watching seven hours of television a day. And then suddenly you're off at school with all this freedom, and everything is zapped at you all at once—just like that—and it goes inside your head and gets all scrambled up, and you don't know where you're at. But you get over that pretty quick, after the shock wears off."

Most of Offer's students made a gradual and painless transition from adolescence to adulthood, from dependence upon parents to mature independence. And they were helped along by parents who allowed them to move away a step at a time. Such parents exercised their authority and provided guidelines for conduct, but they relinquished that authority in stages. They made sure the kids could fly before they kicked them out of the nest.

Keniston agreed that most young people do mature in that fashion. But some of them obviously have suffered the turmoil of a classic identity crisis, and Keniston suggested these were the ones who passed through his proposed youth stage. While there were many of them, he said, they did constitute a minority—and indeed Keniston referred to them as "clearly an elite." He added his opinion that the mental stress was good for them and would lead to a richer adult life.

We will postpone an evaluation of that opinion. Meanwhile, it is worth noting that the identity crisis is not exclusively an affliction of the young. Discussing this point, Andrew M. Greeley said:

"That's one of the interesting things that came up this year in my course on the sociology of religion. I was talking about the religious aspect of the adolescent identity crisis. That is to say, that in order to discover who you are—if you follow Erikson's view—you must also discover what you believe in. And I said in passing that some people think the crisis of the middle years is even more serious and a more difficult crisis to survive. And if you do survive it, you've got twenty or twenty-five happy and productive years ahead of you. And if you don't, you just atrophy. But I told my students: 'That's more of a concern to me than to you.'

"All kinds of hands went up, and all the kids wanted to talk about the crisis of the middle years. And I said: 'What in hell, if there's anybody in the room who's in the crisis it's me. Why does this interest you?' Well, it came out they're all afraid of it. They're afraid they're going to make decisions now—

about career, about marriage, about children—that are going to make it impossible for them to cope with the crisis of the middle years. And I said: 'How come you know about this crisis?' And they said: 'Our parents are all going through it.'

"These are kids with parents in their middle-forties. They're the products of modern families in which there's this closeness between parents and kids, and when the parent has a problem the kid knows about it; not just vaguely, but specifically. 'My parent thinks now his life is wasted. I don't want to make decisions that would put me in the same situation.' So they're very afraid to make any decision. It's essentially a loss of nerve—and a very conservative sort of thing in the sense that you don't want to do anything for fear you might do something irrevocable. Better not to make a decision than to make a decision you won't be able to live with when you're 40. And I told the kids: 'I can talk about this crisis because I think I'm going through it, and there's no way you can really prepare for it. The only way you can prepare for it is to make some commitments, to have some convictions, and live your life—and when the crisis comes, stick to those commitments.' Because that's what the crisis comes down to: 'Was it all worth it?' And middle-aged people are asking if anything they've done or anything they do is worth anything. And if you don't do anything, the crisis is much worse than if you have done something."

So parents and their children share some of the same fears, as well as the same values. And if there is a generation gap today, it is a traditional one. The young, after all, have to establish their own adult identities, and in that process there is certain to be some friction between the young people and their parents. But there also is a bridge across the gap that reaches over to the generation on the other side: to those senior citizens who are the grandparents of the young.

It has been pointed out that demographic trends are shifting; the baby boom peaked in 1957, and the percentage of young people in the total population has started to decline. At the same time, the percentage of old people is increasing. According to some forecasters, this might move the focus of public attention away from young people and the values they express.

But many of these values also are those of the old people.

What the son wants to forget, it has been said, the grandson wants to remember. Literary rebellions, for example, characteristically have repudiated the father and have turned for their inspiration to the previous generation; to the grandfather. And it has been suggested that the life style of today's youth represents an idealization of the Victorian-Edwardian grandfather with his whiskers and muttonchops and handlebar mustache. Which might explain why so many young men today look like the Sundance Kid.

The young and old share more values than is generally recognized. During the initial escalation of the Vietnam War, for example, pollsters found a higher percentage of doves among the old than they did even on college campuses.

The two generations have in common the fact that both have almost no real power to influence society or their own destinies. In America, middle-aged people have most of the power. One possible reaction to this situation might be a political coalition of the young and the old. And in fact a number of organizers and social activists are now working on that project.

Watch out, Dad.

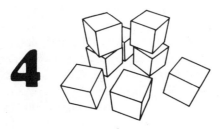

4

Tony, a genial, pleasantly rotund man of forty, falls into a trap. He is asked how he deals with his daughter and, when he answers, finds he is surrounded by a tribe of young, anti-authoritarians.

Tony:	*I openly show affection for my children and I make it a point to sometime in the conversation with them, to tell them that I love them, and not just using lip service, but doing little things for them, something that they dig. And I try to do things with them, but at the same time when they do something that displeases me or I think they're being greedy or not thinking about others, I discipline them. Not physically. I think you achieve more by love and affection. Instead of getting emotional and screaming at them, just sit down and rap with them a little. And I think in talking in a level voice, like I am to you, and explaining why you are displeased and what the penalty is going to be. I don't want them to sit there and shudder when I'm talking to them.*
Yablonsky:	*Do you have any daughters?*
Tony:	*Oh yes. Two.*
Yablonsky:	*Tony, what's your position in regard to your daughter?*
Tony:	*We talk things over and the ultimate decision is really going to be mine. But I try to bring her to my decision. I think at her age now—15—if I haven't done the right job when she's much younger, the ball game's over now. If I haven't raised her right then she may turn into a promiscuous girl.*
Yablonsky:	*What would be promiscuous?*
Tony:	*Oh, in having a sexual relationship before she's married.*
Yablonsky:	*That would be promiscuous?*
Tony:	*I would consider it so.*
Burt:	*I'm afraid that Tony is really making it hard on himself and*

	his daughter. He is setting up such a high standard, a standard that I seriously doubt whether he lives up to in his own life.
Tony:	*I'm trying to keep her away from fellas like you!*
Burt:	*I think that he's establishing a really dynamite situation that's gonna explode. You are going to be disappointed in her because you set your standards much too high. I mean beyond the human capacity, I think.*
Tony:	*Well, you see, maybe I figure she's gonna run into a lot of fellas like me when I was her age. I don't trust them.*
Yablonsky:	*It's okay for you but not for her?*
Tony:	*Sure, of course, of course.*
Mary Ellen:	*Something you said earlier is clicking together and I don't like the way it's going. You said that when you talked to your daughter you usually have the last say, right? In other words, the two of you talk but it's usually what you feel that comes out and you get her to feel that way, right? Like in her problems, it's your decision to bring her along to your decision.*
Tony:	*Not always. But as a rule, I think I know what is better for her.*
Mary Ellen:	*O.K., with that idea in mind, I wonder if you'd allow her to develop qualities in herself to be responsible for what she decides. Is she capable of making her own decisions without being influenced?*
Tony:	*Very definitely, and I do let her make decisions.*
Mary Ellen:	*I think that's really important that all teens are given enough room to experiment with things that they have to decide about, and you accept the failure and learn.*
Tony:	*Don't get the impression that I ride herd on her 24 hours a day. I may talk with her once in two weeks. I see maybe something's happened and I just sit down and talk to her. Like I say, at her age the ball game's over; you just sit back and see what you sowed.*

4.
Alone, With No Excuses

Freedom is probably the most cherished American value, and also the most terrifying. It is the ultimate goal and the ultimate horror. The tension between freedom and authority is the fundamental dynamic in generational conflict and the political antagonisms of a democratic society.

Listen to a 19-year-old Northwestern University coed who appears to be suffering the kind of identity crisis that Kenneth Keniston has said will enrich her adult life. If she belongs to an elite segment of the youth population, she does not seem to appreciate the fact.

"This new psychology that came out when my generation was born," she says, "this thing of don't discipline your children, or don't deny them what they want. As you get older, you find that less and less your parents will say anything constructive. Because parents have read so much. Or else they just don't care, and are willing to let you find out for yourself.

"I can't get the time of day out of my nondirective parents. And believe it or not, but a lot of kids take this as meaning . . . well, you know. I see my friends' parents telling them to do things. Does that mean my parents don't love me? So you develop insecurity and aimlessness and inability to make a decision. I met kids at school last year—juniors and seniors—who had no idea what they were going to do when they got out. They spent $20,000 on college, and they've got no idea what they're going to do. When you're starting out and you're 17 or 18, people say: 'Well, don't worry about it, you've got a year or four years or whatever to decide what you want to do.' And you say, 'Yeah, I'll wait. I'll just mess around.' And pretty soon the four years are up. And you're out.

"And you'd be amazed at the number of people who, despite the freedom of society and the freedom of college, are really hung up about sex, for example. They do a headcount at the age of 20 or 18 and say: 'My God, I've slept with such-and-such a number of people. What am I doing?' And guidance counseling is very helpful. But the kid in the long run has to go back to her room, or the person she can really talk to, and just hash it out and say: 'Okay, I'm going to make a few decisions. I'm not going to accept this idea whatever I want is good.' This thing that parents and teachers have about not channeling the person, and letting your creative interests blossom. That can be so unsettling."

(Thus the question that has been attributed to a child attending a progressive education school: "Teacher, *must* we do today what we want to do?")

A similar view at a different level was expressed by Kevin Starr.

"We abandoned too many orthodoxies in the 1960s," he said. "And I don't see any practical results, except a lot of wasted kids. Can you take the terror of abandoning any relationship to career, to the state, to the political process, to rationality? I mean, how many things can you discard before you have a massive nervous breakdown? Which is just what we had in this country at the end of the decade. I think we're coming out of it now, on the campus at least, and I don't know what way we'll go next. But maybe we'll develop some neo-orthodoxies."

"I'd predict a rebellion against irony," said Hayden White, who is a Marxist and a professor of history at the University of California at Los Angeles. "I'd predict a neo-romanticism. I know that my students at least are fed up with irony in literature, skepticism in thought, and relativism in morality: things that too many people finally pushed to a point of exhaustion."

In psychoanalytic literature, the realm of absolute freedom is the id, which is dominated by the pleasure principle. Authority is represented by the ego, which is dominated by the reality principle, and by the superego or conscience.

Freud said an individual at birth has only an id and is preoccupied with his internal sensations; the id has no awareness of external reality, and it demands instant gratification of its two primary desires, which are the avoidance of pain and the prolongation of pleasure. But the individual gradually develops an ego, or an awareness of external reality, and his ego teaches him there are times when pain must be endured and pleasure must be deferred. He also develops a superego, or the internalized authority of his parents, and the superego dictates the moral limits of behavior within which he can comfortably allow himself to seek pleasure and avoid pain.

Spiro T. Agnew and other psychological reductionists have tended to equate youthful rebellion against authority with permissive childcare, suggesting that demand feeding and similar indulgences produce id-dominated individuals who have underdeveloped egos and superegos, and consequently a low tolerance for frustration. But this reading of the situation was disputed, at the climax of the Movement, by a number of respected psychiatrists including Jarl E. Dyrud and Daniel X. Freedman.

"I don't think these kids grow up with weak egos," said Dyrud. "I think they grow up with punishing superegos. Everybody talks about this new youth—so free, so happy. Well, these permissively raised kids have had to develop their own internal constraints on their behavior—and these are a great deal more rigid and punishing than the average good parent would have given them, if he had taken the trouble to set limits. The good parent sets limits. He helps the child define reality. This means that the child is provided with a problem-solving range, between those limits, that is appropriate to his skills. If this happens, he moves from success to success with a growing sense of well-being and personal competence, and he is never placed in a disastrous situation where the problems are beyond his capacity of solution."

"These untempered attitudes you see today" said Freedman, "come from a lack of authentic autonomy tested out by a sequence of developmental experiences whereby your inner vision of what you are and what others are is modified. The most authoritarian people are those who either see the world as a conspiracy in which they are helpless or are ready themselves to impose upon the world a bunch of super-strict behaviors. We're talking about aberrant developments of the superego, and you see this now in these kids who won't listen. Because they *know* they're right. What they're really engaged in, however, is moral masochism, and moral sadism."

Rebellion against authority in fact may sometimes represent a fear of too much freedom, or indeed a desperate and pathetic plea for authority to impose some kind of limits on the individual's behavior: "For God's sake, how far do I have to go before you stop me?" The analyst Bruno Bettelheim, for example, has observed this phenomenon in some of the troubled young people he has treated at the Sonia Shankman Orthogenic School.

"That's right," he said. "They ask for the limits. I'm running a treatment institution. I've been running it for a quarter of a century. And I know that what all young people need is certainly understanding, certainly gentle handling, but within firm limits. Because, as one of my delinquents said after we had cured him, he said: 'You can't grow up if there are no walls to push against.' And then, after a thought, he said: 'But you can't grow up either if the walls give way when you push against them.' "

To return to the point raised by Starr and White, what happens to a society that abandons virtually all of the limits represented by culture and tradition—as we in this country appeared to have done during the last decade? One result, according to Edward T. Hall, was our obsessive fascination with public-opinion polls.

"We paid a price when we overthrew our institutions," said Hall. "Living is such a complicated business that you can't possibly learn to do it in a lifetime, starting from scratch as it were. Because it takes generations to develop solutions to some human problems, and no human being can live without some ties to the past. But we threw out all the models—all the traditions of our fathers and grandfathers—and nothing was stable any more. So we turned to the polls and tried to build a country on surveys and public opinion, because they provided us with some measure of certainty.

"But they didn't work. Because polls are feedback systems, and a feedback system has certain characteristics. And one characteristic is that if you monkey with it too much, you throw it into a very unstable condition in which it begins to fluctuate wildly back and forth. Because the feedback is so fast, and in the attempt to control it you end up overcontrolling it. It's like overcontrolling an airplane, when a gust lifts a wing. The swings get bigger and bigger, and every time you put a control on it swings back more the other way. And this is what's happening now in television programming and in marketing and in politics—because in addition to everything else we're also packaging politicians now on the basis of public-opinion polls. So everything we have now looks alike—our cars and our politicians—because we've discarded experience and human judgment, and we're captives of a system that nobody controls."

Some people turned not to polls but to youth, mythologizing the Now Generation: adult groupies—the campfollowers of the young—who put on bells and tinted glasses and gave up their tragic centers. They turned to people like Abbie Hoffman, who offered this vision of a free society:

"We will fly the flag of nothingness over the Pentagon, and a mighty cheer of liberation will echo through the land. 'We are Free, Great God Almighty, Free at last.' Schoolchildren will rip out their desks and throw ink at stunned instructors, office secretaries will disrobe and run into the streets, newsboys will rip up their newspapers and sit on the curbstones masturbating, storekeepers will throw open their doors making everything free, accountants will all collapse in one mighty heart attack, soldiers will throw down their guns. 'The War is over. Let's get some ass.' No more permits, no *N.Y. Times* ads, no mailing lists, no meetings . . . Extend all boundaries, blow your mind."

That flag, of course, was the black flag of anarchy (basic black, in fashion for a time), and there also were those who identified instead with the red flag of the SDS and other pseudo-Marxist cadres. But the American masses did not want a Revolution, cultural or political, and only a profound ignorance of modern history could have convinced anybody that this country was ripe for one. Revolutions in this century have occurred only in underdeveloped societies with peasant and lumpenproletariat majorities who lived in such desperate conditions they had almost nothing to lose in smashing the existing order and authority (except of course their chains, which in most cases were merely exchanged for new chains). If a Revolution were possible in an industrialized Western society, it would have occurred in the defeated nations of Europe after World War I. And indeed the Bolsheviks in Russia were confident there would be a "German October" very soon after the armistice. But that did not happen. And according to Antonio Gramsci and other Communist theorists, it did not happen because the working class felt it had too much to lose in the destruction of a highly-complex culture, even in shattered Germany. How much more unlikely, then, was the possibility of Revolution in the post-industrial America of the 1960s.

In fact, the revolutions that did occur were seen to produce not more freedom but less, resulting as they did in the emergence of a new class of bureaucratic leaders who were even more ruthless than the capitalists in extracting the surplus value from labor. And while many Americans were convinced of the need for drastic social change in this country, our own would-be revolutionaries did not inspire much confidence that their leadership would lead to democratic vistas and an increase in liberties.

"Some of these guys should've been on the payroll of the John Birch Society," said Saul Alinsky. "I remember back in the 1930s, in the CIO days. We'd have a strike meeting to compel an employer to recognize the union, and one of these finks on the company payroll would get up and say: 'What's all this crap about negotiating and striking and getting a contract? Let's burn the joint down.' That's exactly what the employers wanted. And that's exactly what the Weathermen and some of these other guys were doing, a lot of them. You got a lot of people who were not in on a social cause but were out doing their own thing. They were rolling for revelations, not Revolution. Real divine miracles that suddenly come down. And values will be changed.

"In a real revolutionary situation, most people have disengaged from past values. They don't know what new values to follow; all they know is, the past isn't working any more. They're confused. And at that point a revolutionary party comes in and says: 'This is the program—this way.' And most people will not be for them. But they won't be against them—what I call a positive passivity. 'We won't get in it. But we won't buck it.'

"There was a so-called reformation period where this was happening in this country, and people were starting to wonder about things. And then came all the violence, and the bombs. And I saw the reaction of these middle-class people, and the reaction was: 'We know what we had in the past wasn't working. But my God, if this is going to be the new way—we've got to go back and get it working. We can't buy this.'

"And whose fault was it, what happened? My generation should have said to these kids: 'Hey, stop it, for Christ's sake. You want your goddamn diapers changed. You don't know what the fuck you're doing.' And I said it. But nobody else would say it. Because they were getting so age-conscious they were scared to death the kids would turn on them and say: 'Boy, you're not with it. You're just over the hill. You belong in another world.' "

But the kids Alinsky talked about were a minority, and they were not even successful in selling their ideas to their peers.

"The SDS people were not very good salesmen," said a student editor at Harvard. "They often violated human decency and the sort of vague set of values you'd been brought up with, and they didn't present themselves as very likeable people when they talked to you, at least on political things. They'd tell you: 'You must listen to me.' For most students, the ultimate value is freedom, human freedom, and the SDS would take this vulgar Marxist line and insist on it. And I think the students' eventual reaction was that SDS's pontification was a threat to their own individual freedom."

If the appeal of the law-and-order issue often had racist overtones, it also reflected what may well have been an even more basic desire to re-establish at least some sense of continuity and normalcy in a faddish culture that had junked too much of its own past. If law with justice was a more properly balanced concept, the same might be said of freedom with order. To crave a measure of order, after all, is simply to crave sanity, as opposed both to the anarchy of schizophrenia and the psychotic determinism of paranoia.

But freedom is a bitch goddess, and there are those who would reject her favors, preferring certainty over liberty. At the deepest level—which is the level of pathology—the love of authority is expressed in the two forms of human aggression: the internalized and the externalized, or masochism and sadism. Those may be two sides of a coin, but Freud in his later period decided that all aggression in fact was the product of a primary masochism, which he identified in turn with the concept of a death instinct (or Thanatos) that conflicts in man's nature with the life instinct (or Eros). Norman O. Brown, extending that theory, proposed that the sado-masochistic complex—negative and positive authoritarianism—results from repression of the death instinct and man's refusal to accept the fact he is an animal who lives and dies. Unable to accept death, he also in consequence is unable to live a free and healthy life.

A common root for masochism and sadism was postulated by Erich Fromm, a neo-Freudian, in his classic study *Escape from Freedom*. Fromm argued that both result from man's sense of aloneness and powerlessness in modern industrial society. The masochist tries to eliminate that burden of aloneness (freedom) by losing his sense of individual selfhood. And he seeks to lose it by becoming part of a larger whole—which may be another person, an institution, a political movement, or God. The sadist desires complete mastery over another person or persons, and for the identical reason: because of his inability to bear the isolation of his individual selfhood, and the necessity to achieve union with some other self "in such a way as to make each lose the integrity of its own self and make them completely dependent on each other." Masochists in fact may sometimes appear to be rebels who defy authority, but only because the existing authority arouses their contempt by any display of weakness. "Such persons might fight against one set of authorities, especially if they are disappointed by its lack of power, and at the same time or later on submit to another set of authorities which through greater power or greater promises seems to fulfill their masochistic longings." Which explains why "radical" libertarians often shift inexplicably to extreme authoritarianism. "The authoritarian character loves those conditions that limit human freedom, he loves being submitted to fate."

But some people believe that there is no human freedom—that man in effect is a machine or a biochemical physical system that responds in a predictable manner to external stimuli; that he has no free will and is incapable of independent action; that his behavior can be conditioned by aversive controls and positive reinforcers, or by punishments and rewards. The most prominent exponent of this view is the behavioral psychologist B. F. Skinner, who asserts it is impossible to change people or society by appealing to the so-called inner man, because there is no inner man. "We shouldn't try to change people," he said. "We should change the world in which people live. You don't change the way a person feels by changing something inside him. You change his environment. And then that of course will change the way he feels. If you say this is an age of anxiety, for example, and we've got to alleviate people's anxieties, that's wrong. This is an age in which all kinds of things are happening—war, pollution, the possibility of atomic holocaust—and these are the things that cause the behavior and make people anxious. So you don't try to alleviate the anxiety by changing people or something inside the person. What you ought to do is create a more peaceful world."

Skinner favors nonaversive controls and resents the suggestion that his theories inspired the movie *Clockwork Orange,* but considerable controversy followed the publication of his latest book *Beyond Freedom and Dignity*. Discussing a *Time* magazine review of the book, he said: "*Time* said I said we can't afford freedom. I never said any such thing. I want people to be as free as they've ever been, and in fact a lot freer—in the sense that they have escaped from punitive, coercive, abusive controls. I want people to *feel* free. But the mistake is to think that when you feel free you are. Because you're not. You're just behaving for different kinds of reasons, and it's very dangerous to overlook that. When you do what you want to do, you feel free. But why do you want to do it, you see?"

The criticisms of behavioral conditioning are too complex to deal with here, but Mark Twain made an observation that may be pertinent: "We should be careful to get out of an experience only the wisdom that is in it—and stop there; lest we be like the cat that sits down on a hot stove-lid. She will never sit down on a hot stove-lid again—and that is well; but also she will never sit down on a cold one anymore." And the British psychiatrist R. D. Laing, in a barb that may well have been aimed at Skinner, asked why a person who says that men are machines may be regarded as a great scientist, while an individual who insists that he himself is a machine is considered a depersonalized schizophrenic. I asked Skinner his reaction to that, and he replied: "Well, Laing is very clever with words, of course."

Also opposed to the Skinnerian thesis are such existentialists as Jean-Paul Sartre, who asserts that man—to his dismay—has absolute freedom: a freedom to make his blood run cold. His existence precedes his essence. Which means, said Sartre, "that, first of all, man exists, turns up, appears on the scene, and, only afterward, defines himself." In the beginning is subjectivity; in the beginning, man is nothing. "Only afterward will he be something, and he himself will have made what he will be. . . . Man is nothing else but what he makes of himself." There is no God to guide him along his evolutionary path. There is no such thing even as an inherent "human nature" or biological plan that will determine the course of his growth. He is born free; he is indeed "condemned to be free" and "condemned every moment to invent man." He is alone, with no excuses. And it is this conviction that makes Sartre want to vomit.

If he is right, it follows that a land of the free must also, of necessity, be the home of the brave.

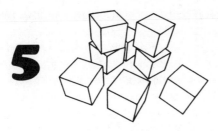

5

Linda is twenty-three, divorced, and the mother of a two-year old boy. She has to decide how to care for herself and her child and in an improvised television meeting she discusses her situation with her father.

Dad:	*Would you like to come home and stay with us?*
Linda:	*I can't, Dad. I would be very uncomfortable in your home after six years of being away. We've got different worlds. I'm moving into a house with a lot of other people.*
Dad:	*What kind of people?*
Linda:	*Both men and women.*
Dad:	*What do you mean, 'both men and women'?*
Linda:	*Both men and women! We've got a house that's sort of like yours and Mom's only bigger with more rooms. They're good people. They're warm and loving people.*
Dad:	*Are these people married?*
Linda:	*Some of them are. Some of them aren't.*
Dad:	*What are you gonna gain by living with these people than living with us?*
Linda:	*I gain my freedom by living there.*
Dad:	*Would you have a better chance of getting a job by living in this commune?*
Linda:	*No, probably worse.*
Dad:	*All right. So what do you gain by this?*
Linda:	*I gain the ability to live inexpensively with people who care about . . .*
Dad:	*It would be inexpensive living with us.*
Linda:	*No, the cost would be too great.*
Dad:	*And what would that cost be?*
Linda:	*The cost to me would be to give up my freedom, to give up*

	my individuality, to become once again your daughter, instead
	of me.
Dad:	*You mean if you lived with us you wouldn't be you? You'd*
	be somebody else?
Linda:	*I could be 20, 25, or 30 and if I were living with you I would*
	still be your little girl. I have to grow up and I have to do this
	on my own. Can't you give me a chance and see if this will
	work?
Dad:	*I can see why you want to be on your own.*
Linda:	*And I can swing it better this way.*
Dad:	*You can swing it better but not by living in a commune.*
Linda:	*What's the matter, Dad? Don't you trust me?*
Dad:	*It's just that I'm concerned for you. I want you to be here*
	where I can help you. I want you to do what's right. I want
	you not to be in the position where you may be forced to make
	a decision that may hurt you.
Linda:	*You have a family but I have adopted another family. I choose*
	to live with another group of people.
Dad:	*You consider that as a family? What kind of responsibilities*
	do you have to each other?
Linda:	*I have an understanding of individuals I am living with that*
	trust the responsibility that each one has or else I would not
	have chosen that particular group. You see with all these
	people around they can help me, where if I were in an apart-
	ment by myself I would have to . . .
Dad:	*You're living with other people that are transients. They come*
	and go.
Linda:	*I think the difference between what you're saying about com-*
	munal living and what I feel is that the contemporary family
	is too narrow in scope. Like where are all the aunts and uncles
	that used to be? I think that like our situation is providing like
	extended family and that's really important.

After she moves in, Linda finds that a commune has its own family problems.

Linda:	*Rick, there is something I want to talk with you about. I'm*
	primarily concerned about the initial agreement we had that
	there would be no dope in the house.

Rick:	*Well, what gives you the idea that I'm breaking the agreement?*
Linda:	*There were joints in the ashtray in the living room.*
Rick:	*What are you so uptight about? Like I know we have a rule and all that stuff, but rules are made to be broken. What do you have against dope anyway?*
Linda:	*I have a two year old son and if you leave joints in the living room he's going to eat them and I don't want him . . .*
Rick:	*Let him eat some and find out what it's like. Maybe it will do something for him.*
Linda:	*Like brain damage, maybe? If this is going to continue and you're going to take that position, I gotta get out of here because I'm concerned about my son. I'm concerned about Matthew eating stuff and I'm concerned about the house getting busted.*
Rick:	*What are you really hung up about? You just want to protect your kid.*
Linda:	*We've got to come to some agreement that there is no dope so I can stay. If you want the dope, I've got to go.*
Rick:	*Why are you so uptight about us?*
Linda:	*I think if you guys are going to want to do dope or ball people in the living room it's your business. Just let me know so I can keep my kid out of your way.*
Rick:	*Well, what's the matter with that? What's the matter with making love in the living room?*
Linda:	*That's impinging upon my privacy. You're co-opting the choices of all the people in the house.*
Rick:	*It's a crazy world, baby. You gotta make do somehow.*

5.
Communes and Technology

Reports of the death of the nuclear American family appear to have been greatly exaggerated. The traditional family structure seemed to be falling apart during the 1960s, when we saw a multitude of efforts made by people in this country to achieve an extension of intimacy: the communal movement, the encounter groups, the tribal mystique of the Woodstock Nation. But the current may well have reversed its direction, and many of the signs now point toward a significant reduction of intimacy. One-to-one personal relationships are increasingly preferred to identification with groups, communes, communities, or collectives, and young people in particular are expressing a renewed and indeed an intensified interest in the values of family life. What some social observers have interpreted as a destructive assault upon that institution may in fact represent a desperate attempt to rescue and restore it.

From the viewpoint of some social activists, a family revival would be unfortunate. There appears to be an inherent antagonism between familial loyalty and social solidarity, and it can be traced back to the emergence of the modern family structure in the seventeenth century.

Erich Fromm and others have argued that mankind historically has evolved in the direction of increased individualism and increased alienation from society; that man in the Middle Ages thought of himself not as an individual but as part of an organic society, and that individualism did not develop until the Reformation and the rise of capitalism. Philippe Ariès in turn has related the withdrawal from society to the evolution of the family, which occurred during the same period and which corresponded with the invention of childhood and formal education (see Chapter Three).

Ariès pointed out, for example, that family scenes are seldom found in the art of the sixteenth century, and that the scene most frequently depicted is the crowd: "not the massive, anonymous crowd of our overpopulated cities, but the assembly of neighbors, women and children, numerous but not unknown to one another." Public life predominated almost to the total exclusion of personal privacy, and the typical house resembled a hippie crash pad; designed for communal living, it was open to callers around the clock, and people lived together in all-purpose rooms (the curtained bed one of the few concessions to privacy). But the next century saw the development of the nuclear family unit—father, mother, and children—and the new concept of family life either satisfied or contributed to a new craving for privacy: "it reinforced private life at the expense of neighborly relationships, friendships, and traditional contacts." It also created a new class consciousness in which the middle class divorced itself from the lower class, "withdrew from the vast polymorphous society to organize itself separately, in a homogeneous environment, among its families, in homes designed for privacy, in new districts kept free from all lower-class contamination." Ariès concluded that "sociability and the concept of the family were incompatible, and could develop only at each other's expense."

The family's retreat from society continued, and after World War II the move to new districts in America became the flight to the suburbs. The result was the rootless, highly-mobile postwar suburban family that anthropologist Margaret Mead has described as "totally isolated, desperately autonomous." A family with "no grandparents, no cousins, no neighbors, no nothing." And it was this kind of family that produced the kind of reaction we saw in the last decade: the search for a sense of community and the proliferation of communal-living experiments.

For many, the search continues. But the communal movement appears to have collapsed, and students especially seem to be disenchanted with it. At Harvard, an economics major said: "People wanted to identify with some kind of group, I guess, but they found out they didn't really get along that well together. The therapy didn't work, and they moved on to other things. For one thing, there's the division of labor in communal living. As an economist, I think that's a very significant factor. It produces severe alienation, in the same sense that Marx talked about in the labor force and society as a whole."

An Antioch College coed related the failure of communes to a decline in sexual promiscuity and the return to a more traditional pattern in male-female relationships. "It used to be a chick-a-night kind of thing," she said. "Or a guy-a-night. But it seems lately that more people are settling down and finding one person they like. And those two people decide they're going to help each other and shield each other and face the world together. Communes were all right for a month or two, maybe, but spend twelve months out of the year in one and you'd go crazy. You have to get out and find out who you are again. Because the group in a way has become your identity, which isn't really you. And unless the needs of the group are almost identical, you're going to have problems. There are bound to be people who aren't as free sexually as others, for example, and this is going to mess people up a little—the fact they're sleeping with six or seven persons."

Bruno Bettelheim, in his study of the Israeli kibbutzim, found that the closeness and total lack of privacy in those communes seem to produce a collective ego and superego—and, in consequence, an almost overwhelming pressure upon the individual to conform to the will of the group. There is indeed "no way to escape the group." Bettelheim said that the kibbutz tends to create what he referred to as a "flat personality" and offers little opportunity for self-expression, that it is not the kind of environment, for example, from which great art is likely to spring. In a comparable assessment of her own communal experiences, the Antioch coed said:

"It just invariably happens. Everybody in the group has a specific job to do—the division of labor—but all of these people also have different needs and interests, like music or dancing or theater. And so what's going to happen? They'll have to go outside the group to satisfy those needs and enjoy those interests. Or maybe they'll try to make it up within the context of the group. And maybe the group isn't going to reciprocate and be receptive to all this. And it's a strange kind of tension. You're saying this group is going to be your identity, and outside the group you have no identity. But inside the group you can't grow, and you can't change; you certainly can't change with a group as easily as you can change with one person at least. So now you find that one person, to grow with and change with."

"There's no question about it," said Michael Wadleigh. "Communes are falling apart. It was like an adolescent phase we went through, and in our culture people just couldn't take it. In this culture, the boy and the girl want to belong to each other; they want to have loyalty, fidelity, holding hands, and one-to-oneness, so to speak. It's been thoroughly drummed into all of us. And so Woodstock is over, I guess, and where we are now—what we've gone back to—is Erich Segal and *Love Story*."

Bettelheim was told in fact that kibbutzniks regard a boy-and-girl twosome (or any twosome, including a simple friendship) as something alien and a threat to the solidarity of the group. The group does all in its power to break up such twosomes, and invariably succeeds. The young people then settle back again "into a group life that is devoid of true intimacy, though it remains intensely close." And therein lies the ultimate irony of kibbutz society, which was consciously organized to promote an extension of intimacy by overcoming social alienation and too much family closeness. In their own way, the kibbutzniks too are a lonely crowd.

And what of the commune children who are reared collectively by a group of parents? Erich Segal, of all people, has endorsed this practice, on the theory that if two heads are better than one, "twelve hearts to love a child are better than two." But it doesn't seem to work out that way. Describing a visit to the Rainbow Farm commune in Oregon, for example, David Bromwich observed that the children there were given a great deal of freedom but very little love. And how do you free a five-year-old child? When he asks for attention, you tell him: "Fuck off." You tell him: "Fuck off, don't hang around me all day, stay on your own trip." Writing in *Dissent* magazine, Bromwich concluded: "In retrospect, this treatment of children seems to me the worst thing about Rainbow—the only thing quite tangibly evil, because it was more than *self*-destructive." That has been my own observation, in the more anarchistic communes I have visited, and there is a comparable element even in the carefully-structured kibbutzim. Bettelheim remarked upon the kibbutznik's "incredibly deep attachment to nature," and said he would often find a kibbutz child standing alone in contemplation by some favorite landscape: a pond or lake, a hill, a glen. And Bettelheim could not help thinking of Mother Earth and wondering "if the kibbutz-born was trying to find in nature an undemanding acceptance that was absent from his childhood where there were always those demands that come with living forever with others.

Another tangible and obvious evil is the tendency of some communal groups to form around charismatic spiritual leaders who often viciously exploit their young followers. Charles Manson was an extreme case, but not, unfortunately, a unique character type. As an old acquaintance who heads several communes told me, when I suggested a certain similarity, "That's right, I'm exactly like Charlie. The only difference is, I don't kill people."

There are of course many kinds of communes, including sophisticated communities that have formed around such growth-and-learning centers as the Esalen Institute and others that are little more than co-op housing arrangements. But the most interesting in many ways have been the small anarchistic communes of the counterculture, and especially the numerous back-to-the-land rural farming communes. These have represented a serious attempt to establish a permanent alternative to life in America's industrial society, and they have been the living expression of the counterculture's rejection of modern technology. Their fundamental opposition has been not so much to the nuclear family as to the machine and economic materialism. It is necessary, therefore, to discuss the nature of that opposition—and also its validity.

America's young people have condemned their country for fighting two immoral wars, one in Vietnam and one against nature. The second conflict threatens the future of the planet, and public awareness of that fact is one of the lasting contributions of the counterculture that emerged after 1968. Ecology was not even mentioned as an issue in the 1968 political campaigns, and the counterculture deserves much of the credit for inspiring the environmental movement that now questions some of the basic concepts of the industrial society.

Today, the severest critics of technology often are technologists themselves. Some of them indeed have asserted it is necessary to reduce technology and put an end to economic growth. But college students on the other hand tend these days to resist that notion, disputing both the counterculture and the mea culpa technologists, and a majority of them appear now to have discarded the idea that technology as such is inherently evil.

Originally, the agrarian communards and others attacked technology on three levels: metaphysical, philosophical, and pragmatic. Drawing on Asian metaphysics, and psychedelic drug insights, they charged that man's drive to "conquer nature" had alienated him from his own universe; estranged in an artificial existence, he would never be at peace with himself until he learned to live in harmony with nature and stopped the technological tampering that upset the ecological balance of life. Philosophically, it was argued that the technological impulse reflects a neurotic obsession with growth and infinite escalation of the GNP: produce more so you can consume more so you can produce more. Thus man becomes a racing rat who can never stop to enjoy the simple pleasures. The moral: "more is less." Pragmatically, it was pointed out that technology is decaying the quality of life by polluting the atmosphere and despoiling the environment. Worse yet, as social historian Jacques Ellul warned, technology perhaps has become an autonomous force beyond man's control; once set in motion, it reaches a level of complexity where it follows its own blind but inexorable course, a Juggernaut with no brakes or steering wheel.

Such opinions, common a few years ago, are still expressed by some extreme environmentalists. But the campus is no longer a preserve for neo-Luddite machine haters; while ecology is still a major issue, students have developed a more refined view of the problem and the possible solutions. Thus it is argued, for example, that it is in fact the environmentalists who often appear to create the dualism between man and nature; who regard man and all his works as unnatural phenomena; who seem indeed to loathe man, alone of all the creatures on this earth. But man after all is a part of nature, and his creations are simply extensions of his mind. How can anything that exists in nature be unnatural? By what logic is a skyscraper artificial, as opposed to an ant hill or bird's nest or beaver's dam?

Early man moreover was physically an almost helpless animal without fangs or claws to protect him in a hostile environment. His only real weapon was his mind, which provided him with a technology of clubs and spears and firebrands to defend himself from predators, and tampering with his environment was the only way man could possibly survive. Had he chosen to live in ecological harmony, not upsetting the balance of nature, he would have been devoured by saber-toothed tigers. And in those days, the forests belonged to the tigers. As religion professor George Pickering told a technology seminar at Indiana State University: "It is doubtful whether any of the modern experiences of either alienation or powerlessness can equal that for sheer shock. The discovery that the forests belonged to the tigers is simply not in the same class with discovering that the streets belong to the police . . . or even that white people have more power and privilege than they deserve. How our ancestors ever got up the courage to come down from their trees, out from their caves, or wherever it was they came from, and compete with the tigers for possession of the earth is beyond my powers of imagining. Statistically, they did not have a chance."

Today, millions of years later, the odds are still against us. Or so we are told by an elaborate computer study conducted at the Massachusetts Institute of Technology by the international organization that calls itself the Club of Rome. The study suggested that world civilization will collapse within a hundred years unless we stabilize population and stop economic growth. Fossil fuels and other natural resources will be depleted, and the globe will be shrouded in a lethal cloud of pollution.

No responsible authority would deny that a continuation of present trends can lead only to disaster. But student critics of a zero-growth solution point out, for one thing, that the environmental mess is not merely a product of technological development. It also represents a political failure and is equally the product of irrational social policy, as economist John Kenneth Galbraith demonstrated in his study of the affluent society.

Governmental policy has encouraged growth in the private sector of the economy, emphasizing increased production and employment to put more money in the pocket of the individual consumer. By comparison, there has been only a miserly tax investment in the public sector of the economy, in such items as education, mass transportation, urban renewal, welfare, job training, and pollution control. As a result, America is privately affluent and publicly poor. Even a millionaire is poor when he steps out of his mansion into an environment that is ugly and dangerous to life. And students add that major corporations are allowed to establish social policy and national priorities, deciding what they will produce and how they will produce it; they are not even required to pay for the social costs of private production, which include the pollution created by the industrial process.

"We've known this for years," said a University of Chicago economics major. "So the villain isn't only technology. And the fact remains that a lot of people in this country also are privately poor. Then add to that the underdeveloped countries in the Third World, where almost everybody is poor. If you went to Harlem or Chile, I don't think you'd have much luck selling that more-is-less line." To which Eva Scott added: "We black people aren't alienated by technology. We've never had enough of your technology to get alienated by it. We've been too busy surviving."

A panel on technology was held at the 1972 World Affairs Conference at the University of Colorado, in an auditorium jammed with students. A poll of the audience was conducted, and—to the surprise of the moderator—not one student endorsed the concept of trimming technology or freezing economic growth. The students in fact indicated they favored more technology, along with more equitable income distribution and a better system of determining national production priorities.

"It's the only rational way," said one bearded youth, undisturbed by his use of an adjective that in recent years had appeared to be a no-no on many campuses. (*Sic transit Dionysus.*) "I totally agree," said another member of the audience."We can't cut down the economy to benefit people a hundred years from now when most of the world and many Americans are already living in eighteenth-century London. 'I got mine; you can stop right now, Jack.' That's exploitation and elitism." "You could do it," said another student. "But you'd have to have a political revolution first to spread the bread around. Or if you didn't do that first, you'd sure as hell have a revolution on your hands afterwards."

The inventor Buckminster Fuller has insisted the basic cause of war and social unrest is "not enough to go around," and that the only lasting solution to those problems is a superabundant economy, a postscarcity world. That opinion is shared by Michael Harrington, who said: "The goals of socialism certainly depend upon abundance, so I hope at least that the Club of Rome is wrong, and there's an analogy I like that suggests that possibility. Suppose the club had done its study back in 1872. And let's say it made the assumption America would continue to be moved by horsepower. It might then project a 1972 population of more than 200 million people. The experts would ask their computer how many horses we'd need in a hundred years to handle that population, and how much pasturage we'd need to feed all those horses. Then they'd ask the computer another logical question, and announce that the United States by 1972 would be covered by a layer of manure six feet deep. What I'm saying is that the club left out obviously a technological breakthrough. And I think there are possibilities that our dependence on fossil fuels, for example, might be solved by the development of solar energy or tidal energy or geothermal energy."

"That's right," said chemist R. Stephen Berry of the University of Chicago. "The club is assuming we're going to live with the technology we now know.

And what we have to do in a sense is to get rid of the horses and rediscover the automobile."

Berry pointed out the Club of Rome applied highly sophisticated computer models to existing data to confirm something we already know: that we can not pursue our present life style indefinitely. But the study's predictions will hold true only if we do pursue that style. We realize now that we can't. And presumably, therefore, we won't.

Berry himself is currently engaged in an impressive project to study the environmental problem in terms of thermodynamic potential.

This represents the amount of stored energy available to do work. Energy is our fundamental resource; the amount available is finite—we could use it all up—and every use of energy to do work creates wastes. Berry is trying to determine (1) how much energy is available, (2) how much we are consuming, (3) how we can make the most efficient use of energy by practicing "thermodynamic thrift." Such thrift in turn offers three possible alternatives to the zero-growth solution.

The first (short-term) alternative is to maximize recycling, which can consume less energy than manufacturing from ores and other primary materials. According to one estimate, a program of maximum recycling would use about 10 per cent less energy than is presently consumed in the production of a new automobile. To encourage recycling, Berry recommends that a depletion allowance should no longer be paid to people who extract minerals from the earth. Instead, these people should be charged a depletion tax.

The second (intermediate) alternative is to make products that last longer, with much more worker effort devoted to inspection: to increase the quality of production rather than the quantity. For example, the useful life of an automobile might be doubled or tripled. The economic cost would be higher for such extended-life vehicles. But there would be a considerable and ultimately far more important savings in the expenditure of energy, more so than in recycling.

The third (long-range) alternative is to design new technologies that are much more efficient than existing technologies.

"Our manufacturing industries operate far less efficiently than living systems," said Berry. "And if you break down a system like making an automobile into steps, you can pick out those parts that are more efficient and less efficient and say: 'Here's a place where a change in basic technology is possible.' Roughly speaking, living systems operate at an efficiency of a few per cent. Our manufacturing processes on the other hand operate at an efficiency of about 1 to 1,000. In other words, we presently spend about 1,000 times more energy or thermodynamic potential than would be required in a perfectly efficient system. I think we can achieve a reduced ratio of 1 to 100, gaining a factor of 10. We are smart enough that we should be able to gain that factor of 10. And this means we could reduce by tenfold the energy expenditures now necessary to have things. So we don't have to throw up our hands and say we're all going to die if we don't go primitive. That's not a very thoughtful way of doing things."

There is still Ellul's objection, that technology runs itself. And also the objection that technological solutions to a problem tend to create new and greater problems that were unforeseen. But the latter objection would paralyze all human action, if carried to its logical conclusion (as J. Alfred Prufrock asked: "Do I dare to eat a peach?"). And if Ellul's criticisms are valid, which they probably are not, they are certainly not useful.

In the first place, research and development are constantly creating potential technologies. We could never afford to implement all of them with an operational investment, and it is necessary to choose among them. So man does have something to say about the direction technology will take. Every choice he makes precludes some other possibility, and his choices of course are determined by his values. As for Ellul, it is necessary to assume he is wrong when he says technology can not be controlled. If he is right, it makes no difference what we do. But he could be wrong. And if he is, it would be a fatal mistake to accept his philosophy and to abandon all hope and effort.

The counterculture's rural communes are no answer to the problem. That experiment was tried before, in the communitarian movements that swept America in the nineteenth century—Owenism, Fourierism—and that acted if anything as a brake on efforts to achieve radical social change, as Harrington has convincingly argued in his new book *Socialism*. Thus the trade-union movement did not develop until the 1830s, after the failure of Owenism in the previous decade. And the destruction of the labor organizations in the crisis of 1937 was followed by a revival of agrarian radicalism: the dream of free land in the West, where workers could escape the class struggles of industrial capitalism. The spell of free land was so pervasive that socialists were compelled to ally themselves with "pure and simple" trade unionists. And the unions in turn could succeed only in opposition to "middle-class utopians seeking salvation in the fields." Similarly, Marx and Engels rejected the idea that peasant socialism would allow Russia to skip the stage of capitalist industrialization in its dialectical progress toward a classless society, insisting that the realization of this goal depended upon its historic preconditions: an economy of abundance and an enlightened working class. Engels thundered that the isolated communes of the Narodniks created "the very opposite of a common interest" and were "the material basis of Oriental despotism." Peasant socialism indeed has been a base for successful revolution only in nonindustrial countries, such as China, where it has resulted in party dictatorships whose first victims were the peasants themselves; where the peasants were forced off their land into agricultural collectives in which their labor could be

exploited to provide an economic surplus for industrialization. Agrarian uto-
pianism has thus been successful only in creating more technology, as in
China, or in hampering attempts to democratize an advanced technological
society, as in the United States.

If the recent communal movement was an inadequate response to the social
evils of postindustrial technology, it also has failed as an alternative to the
nuclear family. We have said that other efforts are being made to revitalize
the family, as opposed to replacing it, and these will be discussed later when
we examine such subjects as women's liberation and reassessment of the work
ethic. My own experience with young communards suggests that their antagonism to the family is due in many cases to the fact they come from broken or
unhappy homes, and that they have universalized their disappointments to
indict the institution. It would be easy to dismiss them, as Horace Greeley
did their nineteenth-century predecessors, as those who "finding themselves
utterly out of place and at a discount in the world as it is, rashly conclude
that they are exactly fitted for the world as it ought to be." But there is some
fault to be found with the world as it is, after all, and there is something of
substance in the attempt to extend the bounds of intimacy, from personhood
to peoplehood. Consideratioon of this too must be deferred. Meanwhile, if
they have not found utopia, we can hope at least that some of the communards
have found something better for themselves than what they had before. As
Bettelheim said of the kibbutz: "It is a fine system for some and not for
others."

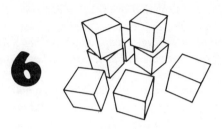

6

Sex is one area where most people can give an informal opinion. The television group met and was bursting with talk.

Freida:	*Well, for most of the young people that I have worked with, a good number of them . . . sex is like a nothing thing. Some have even lived together but I cast no value judgment.*
Lew:	*How do you feel about it though?*
Freida:	*For me, I couldn't do it. I couldn't go to bed with you tonight and him tomorrow night and somebody else. I've got to love you first.*
Lew:	*Sue, how do you feel about that?*
Sue:	*I don't know. I think it has to do with how honest I'm being with myself. It would take a lot out of me to just spend one night with one guy and another night with another guy because I would feel empty inside because there wasn't anything constant in my life.*
Linda:	*All right, but I can see just purely enjoying the release of sex in itself without really feeling. You see, I think that in a way, if you feel that you must love this person, you could almost destroy it for yourself. I think if the two people understand that that's all it is and if it's possible to do something like that, it's O.K.*
Dorothy:	*To me, you pick the person first and then out of this love comes a fulfillment.*
Lew:	*What do you describe as promiscuous?*
Dorothy:	*Sleeping around with anybody just for the fun of the sexual act. And I feel that this is too important a thing for just a physical pleasure.*
Linda:	*I think the sex act can be either of two things. It can be an act*

between two people who genuinely care about each other or it can be an act between two people who may not care about each other so much and are seeking pleasure. There is nothing wrong with the sex act as a pleasure act without a whole background of caring, except that you have to care that the other person is a person but it doesn't have to be an intimacy between the two.

Lew: *What if the possibility of becoming pregnant is no longer an issue? How would you feel about your daughter having sex, Tony?*

Tony: *I'd still be against premarital sex. To be very candid with you, more so for a young girl than I would a fella. I don't know why. Maybe I think they would be taken advantage of.*

Freida: *I used to have a double standard because I always felt that man was the dominant superior and I suppose this had to go along with the fact that men were not going to get pregnant. I've changed that a great deal and I think that sex is a two-way responsibility. If a fella goes to bed with a gal, neither of them are 'out to lunch'. They're both there and therefore they have equal responsibility.*

Barbara: *Apparently, things have really changed and I have really changed and I'm kind of tuning in to what it is really to be a woman.*

Peggy: *Women can do things that men can't do, right? Women can have children. God wanted a nurturing kind of love when he planned the earth and if everybody's supposed to be equal we would have been made the same.*

Barbara: *I hear you denying the fact that men can have nurturing personalities also. It seems like that's a woman's thing—to be nurturing. Is that what you're saying?*

Peggy: *It's a stronger feminine characteristic. Women get a greater deal of satisfaction from this kind of thing.*

Dori: *I think that women are given some free options . . . quite a lot, almost as much as a man is. A man in our society today isn't expected to be weak or sympathetic or show compassion. They're taught when they're little children not to feel this way, not to ever cry, but we're coming out of the dark ages. We realize that a man is capable of all the feelings women are capable of.*

Rob: *Men were brought up to a role they have to live up to. Take John Wayne. You don't cry, you don't kiss anybody, just your horse. I told people one time that I cried in sad movies and*

	afterwards a guy came up and said 'Wow, you've got a lot of guts to admit that'. Men hide their emotions from themselves. I felt I had to.
Judy:	*These are the kinds of things that a parent should present to their children. Also you have to have a trusting kind of relationship and I think that in our society the mother spends most of the time with the child. Why doesn't the father spend an equal amount of time?*
June:	*In other words, you're saying that in the female role that the father should relate to the daughter more than to the son?*
Judy:	*No, equally to both.*
June:	*I think there's something there.*
Barbara:	*I think men and women and society and whatever has happened that men don't deserve any massive blame. They're functioning from a cultural place, too. But I think that if women are free that men are gonna be a hell of a lot freer than they are now.*
Peggy:	*How? In what way?*
Barbara:	*I think that if women are dependent upon themselves that's gonna take an awful lot off a guy that thinks he has to be strong enough for two of you.*
Peggy:	*What's gonna happen to the male when this is taken off? What will they have left?*
Barbara:	*They will have themselves.*
Rob:	*The fact that we have to sit down here and discuss what a man's role should be bugs me because I know I'm a man and I don't have to prove it to anybody.*

6.
Eros Unbound

It has been said that the youth counterculture attracted boys who wanted to be more like girls; that women's liberation attracts girls who want to be men; that the last decade produced a sexual revolution if not a political one, resulting in rampant promiscuity. All of which may be partly true and partly false.

Let us start with something simple, like fornication.

It continues, of course. There may even be more of it than there used to be. Among young people at the college level, however, there appears to have been a recent change in the pattern of sexual relationships. Conclusions on the subject are necessarily impressionistic, since reporters are not invisible and people lie a lot, but students by their own testimony at least have become more conservative in their mating habits. If there is more sexual freedom on campus today, there also is less promiscuity.

"Sex is no longer a big thing," said a graduate student at the University of Chicago. "I don't think there's so much pressure on people to sort of sleep around, and male-female relationships are by and large monogamous. Girl friends are quite faithful to boy friends, and boy friends are faithful too. I know very few girls who are sort of going the rounds. That's not typical behavior anyhow. If you do see a burst of promiscuity, it's basically a sort of disequilibrium phenomenon—as opposed to something you would do over a long period of time."

"The whole sexual revolution business turned out to be a tremendous disillusionment," said a Harvard economics junior. "Maybe one factor was that the revolution became so popular with our parents too. At any rate, there's a feeling among kids now that this idea of sleeping with one girl one night and another girl the next is not such hot stuff. It's really not that interesting, and they don't do it any more. Maybe sleeping with one girl for a couple of months and not getting too attached. That's a different thing. But hopping from bed to bed is not as exciting as it once was."

We have said that the counterculture is dead, in the sense that the middle-class youth population no longer believes that its concepts will lead in the near future to a basic transformation of the nation's political and social structure. In another sense, however, it is alive and sick elsewhere in the society.

"I don't see it in the streets," said Michael Wadleigh. "I don't hear it any more in the music. I don't discover it in the underground newspapers, that's for sure. I don't know where it is—unless it's in the factories now, in a superficial way, and in blue-collar families. I mean, the dope is in the factories. And the young workers are wearing their hair long and look just like hippies—the idea being, I guess, that they couldn't attract the girls otherwise. Even their parents are trying to copy what they think the counterculture was all about, which of course was promiscuous sex. So they sleep around and find it all very titillating. And yet the pathetic thing is, they still basically think that sex is just filthy rotten. It's titillating to the extent that it's forbidden, disgusting, and sort of awful. It's just so weird. In my opinion, these people are going to fucking explode."

If there is less promiscuity on campus at least, this might be due in part to a recognition that the essence of the counterculture to a considerable extent was hedonism—and that hedonists of all people in the world are the easiest to manipulate. Especially sexual hedonists. And some suspicious political militants charged that the establishment had cynically encouraged sexual permissiveness as a social control to keep young people occupied in nonpolitical activity (better bed than red). But it seems far more likely that promiscuity simply became boring—as hedonism usually does, very quickly—and that it failed to satisfy the needs of young people for personal intimacy.

As we saw in the last chapter, attempts to extend intimacy in communal experiments led in fact to less intimacy, and multiplying the number of sexual partners appears to have the same effect. Adult swingers are a case in point. Their mate-swapping orgies invariably are mechanical and passionless affairs in which it is strictly forbidden to display any emotional response higher than biological lust; couples seldom copulate with another couple on more than one occasion, the specific intention of that custom being to avoid emotional involvement, and it is considered an inexcusable breach of etiquette to tell your bed partner: "I love you." For most of us perhaps, being sorry is never having to say that. And our inability to say it sincerely to more than a few people may explain why young people are becoming sexually less democratic.

The quantity of youthful intercourse is much more difficult to judge than its quality. Given the Pill, it would appear inevitable there has been a decrease in premarital virginity. But newspaper articles at least once a month quote social scientists who assure us that their surveys indicate the incidence of intercourse has not increased significantly or at all, that young people are merely much freer today in talking about sex. These surveys of course can not be trusted; there is too much temptation for respondents to fib about their sex habits, one way or the other. But if some young people fear freedom, as we have already suggested, it is not unreasonable to suppose that many of them might be especially fearful of sexual freedom. And that indeed was the pattern Daniel Offer detected in his study (cited earlier) of adolescent boys. Most of them, while in high school, appeared to set very strict limits on themselves and were reluctant to attempt intercourse. "They said they were afraid of getting the girls pregnant," said Offer. "Which is interesting to me, because after all they knew all about contraceptives. So I pressed them on that issue, and that was the only time in my years of experience they became very anxious and kind of angry. Because it was obviously a rationalization. If it wasn't pregnancy it would be venereal disease, and if these two were taken out it would be, you know, because somebody up there didn't like it."

Jarl Dyrud related this sexual reluctance to the adolescent's need for reasonable limits within which to develop his skills and confidence. Referring to the duenna system practiced in Spain, he said: "When a girl goes out on a date, she takes an older woman with her as a chaperon. So the girl then is free to develop her feelings of attractiveness. She's free to enjoy her growing erotic feelings, because there are limits within which she is safe. But we take young people even twelve or fourteen years old and put them in situations which demand extreme self-restraint, so they can't afford to feel and develop seductive behavior. And this is constricting. Take the Pill. By giving adolescents the Pill we are very often depriving them of the chance to develop emotional depth and real texture in their lives. We're saying in effect to go ahead and act on this, at a time when you might appropriately be setting limits."

But enough of fornication. If there really was a sexual revolution in the 1960s, its deeper significance was not the liberation of the genitals but the liberation of the human body as a whole, the liberation of the flesh and senses from the domination of the abstract rational mind. It was a celebration not of genital sexuality, or copulation, but of pregenital infantile sexuality as defined by Freud and apotheosized by Norman O. Brown. In proposing that infants have a sexual life, Freud did not mean to imply they are preoccupied with their genital organs; on the contrary, he suggested they are polymorphously perverse: that they are erotically stimulated by pleasurable sensations emanating from all parts of the body, including the internal organs, and involving the entire sensorium—sight, hearing, smell, touch, and taste. Adult sexuality on the other hand is concentrated in the genitals and represents an unnatural restriction on the erotic possibilities of the human body. And while infantile sexuality responds exclusively to the pleasure principle, adult sexuality is a response to the reality principle—in this case, the necessity to propagate. Sexual foreplay in the adult is a perpetuation of polymorphous perversity— the pure and richest form of sexual pleasure, which is terminated by genital orgasm. Thus the sadness after orgasm: the frustration of the repressed child of delight who remains hidden in all of us.

Freud believed civilization and its discontents were a product of the repression and sublimation of the primitive pleasures—and especially sexual forces—but he also thought civilization was worth those discontents. Brown on the other hand concluded that civilization was a neurosis. As we saw in Chapter Four, he held that sado-masochism and the inability to enjoy life result from man's refusal to accept the fact he is a mortal organism—which is to say, a body. In his influential book *Life Against Death*, published in 1959, he called for the "abolition of repression" and the "resurrection of the body." He wrote: "The life instinct, or sexual instinct, demands activity of a kind that, in contrast to our current mode of activity, can only be called play. The life instinct also demands a union with others and with the world around us based not on anxiety and aggression but on narcissim and erotic exuberance."

That concept, not intercourse, was what the sexuality of the subsequent counterculture was really all about. It meant an affirmation of the body and the senses (enhanced by drugs) and a subjugation of the work ethic to the play ethic. It also meant a rejection of mind, or rationality, since the rational mind was the Trickster that had caused man to forget he was a body. And by a happy coincidence, it was learned that the same drugs that enhanced sensory perception also had the effect of shutting off the rational mind.

The counterculture's aversion to personal hygiene also can be related to Freudian theory; specifically, the theory that the olfactory sense was devaluated when man raised himself off the ground and assumed an erect posture. Freud suggested this led ultimately to "the cultural trend towards cleanliness." He explained: "The incitement to cleanliness originates in an urge to get rid of the excreta, which have become disagreeable to the sense perceptions." This is not true in the nursery, however, and the excreta "arouse no disgust in children." It is parental upbringing (repression) that insists the excreta are disgusting and abominable, resulting in a "reversal of values" that would not be possible "if the substances that are expelled from the body were not doomed by their strong smells to share the fate which overtook olfactory stimuli after man adopted the erect posture." The supposedly unrepressed and polymorphously perverse counterculturalist presumably reversed values again, affirming his excreta and other odors along with the rest of his body. And this line of thought might explain as well the counterculture's affinity for "dirty" words associated with excrement and bodily functions.

(Freud incidentally connected upright posture with the origin of the primitive family, or primal horde. When he loped along close to the ground, with an acute sense of smell, man was sexually attracted to woman primarily during her menstrual period. After he stood up, he was aroused by sight rather than odor. Which meant he could become aroused whenever he saw a woman. The genitals had now become visible, and Freud speculated that this may have led "to the continuity of sexual excitation, the founding of the family, and so to the threshold of human civilization.)

Brown's book had a powerful impact, as did Herbert Marcuse's *Eros and Civilization*. But such books did not create the counterculture; they merely provided it with a rationale and a vocabulary to articulate its philosophy. What created the counterculture, as indicated earlier, were the affluence and leisure of the 1960s, which temporarily suspended the economic reality principle and freed a swollen youth population to respond almost exclusively to the pleasure principle. There also were other influences and other books, including white youth's encounter with black culture during the civil rights movement and Eldridge Cleaver's *Soul on Ice*.

Cleaver asserted the white man in America had come to represent Mind (in the sense of a rational, abstract, scientific approach to life), while the black man had come to represent Body (in the sense of an emotional, intuitive, physical response to life). But the blacks came to the rescue of the whites and reintroduced them to their bodies; Chubby Checker showed them how to dance the Twist, and the white people learned "how to shake their asses again." Cleaver attributed the white man's alienation from his body not to repression but to a preoccupation with technology, and he said man in the machine age needs to reaffirm his biology. "He feels a need for a clear definition of where his body ends and the machine begins, where man ends and the *extensions* of man begin . . . the blacks, personifying the Body and thereby in closer communion with their biological roots than other Americans, provide the saving link, the bridge between man's biology and man's machines."

Black emotional intensity has been said to represent simply short-term hedonism produced by a culture of poverty, but it also has been attributed by other cultural observers to the emotional warmth of the black matriarchal family. And indeed there is a school of thought that suggests the mind-body dichotomy is not a white-black phenomenon but an expression instead of a conflict between patriarchal and matriarchal values.

The basis for this theory was provided in 1861 by J. J. Bachofen, whose studies of Greek mythology convinced him that the worship of the Olympian gods was preceded by a religion in which the supreme deities were mother goddesses. This led him to speculate that the family and society in Western prehistory were originally matriarchal in structure (ruled by the women), since the promiscuity of sexual relationships meant a child's consanguinity could be traced only to the mother, and women were therefore respected as the source of life and law. Later the men took over and imposed a patriarchal structure on the family, society, and religion. Scholars have disputed the notion that a matriarchal religion presupposes a matriarchal family and society, but Erich Fromm and others have nevertheless extended Bachofen's concept to reinterpret the Oedipus myth. Thus for Fromm, "the myth can be understood as a symbol not of incestuous love between mother and son but of the rebellion of the son against the authority of the father in the patriarchal family."

Patriarchy is said to emphasize rationality, order, hierarchy, and obedience to authority. Matriarchy is supposed to symbolize intuition, emotion, and the nurturant qualities of love, unity, and peace. And the youthful values of the counterculture have been interpreted to represent a new rebellion of the sons against the authority of the father and the patriarchal social structure. Thus the long hair, for example, symbolized a rejection of the dominant masculine image and an affirmation of matriarchal humanism. And it is in this context that sympathetic students of the counterculture said that boys wanted to be more like girls—or more like their mothers and less like their fathers. The so-called blurring of sex roles among young people really had nothing to do with physical heterosexuality; it was an expression rather of humanistic social values.

Kenneth Keniston indeed concluded from his studies of the activist-producing family in the 1960s that it tended to focus on an active mother engaged in a professional or service role that expressed a strong "nuturant concern for others." And such a mother typically appeared to have "a dominant psychological influence on her son's development." As a rule in this kind of family, said Keniston, "it is the mother who actively embodies in her life and work the humanitarian, social, and political ideals that the father may share in principle but does not or can not implement in his career." That pattern was confirmed in similar studies by sociologist Richard Flacks, but he found that it was not in fact limited to activist-producing families; he found that "*most* middle-class suburban families today have these characteristics—where the mother is the central figure for the children, and the father is in many ways less central."

The idealization of the nurturant mother is not shared by other authorities who are more inclined to express concern over the downgrading of paternal authority that occurred in suburbia after World War II. Offer, for example, said that his "modal adolescents" originally felt much closer emotionally to their mothers, than to their fathers. By the time they were ready to start college, however, they tended to draw away from their mothers and to identify more with their fathers. Offer suggested that Keniston's warm and humanistic mothers are actually overly involved in their children. "They smother the children and won't let go." They are possessive, and they resist the necessity for their children to separate and establish their own adult identities. And it is the children of such mothers who are most likely to suffer a severe identity crisis. "The mothers in my group were possessive," said Offer, "but they could let go. They don't want to separate, but they know they have to separate. It's very painful for them, and it's very slow: it takes them many years, I think. But they can do it when they have to."

It also is hard for the children to separate, a difficulty analyst Otto Rank traced to the birth trauma (the underlying source of all separation anxiety), which Rank thought results in a perpetual desire to return to the mother. Rank proposed that the function of the father in the primal horde was to prevent the sons from acting on that desire. Patriarchal societies emphasize paternal authority to repress the memory of the birth trauma; but the wish to return to the mother has reasserted itself in various historical periods, resulting in revolutions against masculine dominance.

The son's attitude toward the father is ambivalent. Offer's subjects indeed said they wanted a strong father. "This gives the adolescent not only a worthy adversary but one who can set limits on his strengths," said Offer. "The strict father enables the boy to take responsibility for his own rebellion when he does rebel." And a weak father on the other hand may contribute to acute psychological distress. Bruno Bettelheim said emotionally disturbed radicals he has treated came from families in which the mother was dominant and the father was "real weak in the home." Bettelheim added: "And I think one of the characteristics of those I studied was tremendous anxiety about their masculinity—and therefore through violence, and violent aggression to paternal authority, they try to demonstrate to themselves and to their colleagues that contrary to their anxieties they're really strong he-men."

A number of studies have attempted to learn what happens to a youth population in war periods when there are no at-home models of men available, when fathers are in military service and children during the classical oedipal period are reared exclusively by their mothers. One such study pointed out that the German children who were reared by their mothers during World War I were also the chief supporters of Hitler and Nazi authoritarianism in the early 1930s. Another study suggests that virulent racism in the South did not really exist until the late 1880s and early 1890s, with the coming of age of the young men whose fathers had been off fighting the Civil War. And we have already quoted Edward T. Hall (in Chapter Two) on the possible consequences of World War II to American children whose fathers were in service and whose mothers in addition were often employed in war industries.

Most fathers today may not be at war, but the typical middle-class suburban father is habitually absent: at the office or on the road or commuting for hours between office and home. Even when he is physically present in the house, he has abdicated his traditional role as an authority figure. And the invasion of the work force by women has meant that many children now have not one absent parent but two.

The latter situation presumably will be accentuated in the future if the pop version of women's liberation succeeds. And what that might do to family life and the adolescent psyche is impossible to predict. But women's liberation can not be dismissed on such grounds, because it is a just cause. As a man I know said: "I have heard the cry of pain, and I know that it is real." That is just what it is, a cry of pain, and it is a tragic and brutal insult that so many men apparently are unable either to hear it or to understand it, or worse yet, that they hear it and laugh. I am not an angry man, but that laughter makes me angry. I do not believe that men are monsters, but that laughter makes me wonder.

Erik Erikson, among others, has said it would be a shame if liberation merely results in women becoming like men, and Erikson is among those who have suggested women have a special nurturant capacity that expresses itself in the supposedly matriarchal values we have talked about: love, tenderness, emotion, and compassion. That sounds very nice, but it is patronizing and degrading if it also implies that women do not possess the intellectual capacity that has been assigned to the patriarchs; if it implies, in short, that they do not possess rational minds but only an endearing intuition. "The ladies, God bless them." That is on a par with suggesting they have a natural sense of rhythm and are born tap dancers. They have minds, and they are fighting now for the life of their minds. In doing so, many of them have come to resent the notion of a nurturant capacity that is biologically assigned to them as wives and as mothers. And they resent even more the related assumption that they have no real identity unless they are wives and mothers, or accessories to men. They resent the idea that they need men to be complete human beings. Of course they need men, although some of them in their pain have been inspired to deny it. What is outrageous is the idea that they need men more than men need them; as the song tells us, a man without a woman is like a ship without a sail, but "in the universe/ there's nothing worse/ than a woman without a man."

If men lack a nurturant capacity, it would indeed be a shame if women became like men, and far better that men should become more like women. But hopefully those qualities of love, tenderness, emotion, and compassion are not matriarchal values but human values. And children need them. They need them from mothers *and* fathers. That is what liberation is really about, and we will hear some of the young people talking about this in our final chapter when we examine the future of careerism and the work ethic. The way they are talking about liberation does not imply the destruction of the American family; it could mean its salvation.

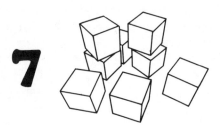

7

Bob is an army officer with combat experience in Korea and Vietnam. He talks with Janice, a girl nearly twenty, about the meaning of patriotism.

Janice:	*I believe in my country. I would be proud to be an American were my country doing what I felt to be the right thing. At the moment I feel my country is killing people . . . it makes me cry what I feel the country is.*
Bob:	*What country would you like to belong to?*
Janice:	*I am a member of this country and that's why I'm working to change it. I don't want to live anywhere else. I want to be here and I want to change it so it can be a place I can live in and I haven't given up yet and if I give up, then I'll leave. I don't want to have to give up and have to leave. I want to see a new country in a new era.*
Bob:	*What then is your definition of patriotism?*
Janice:	*I have a patriotism toward all people . . . towards all human beings . . . a patriotism toward life and not towards any geographical region. I think that you feel that patriotism is supporting your country . . . is nationalism . . . is going with your country no matter what it does but I feel patriotism is the obligation to rectify the wrongs within your country.*
Bob:	*Put it right through bombs?*
Janice:	*Did I ever say anything about violence?*
Bob:	*That's the way your side is.*
Janice:	*Our side's not like that. We haven't killed all the people in Vietnam.*
Bob:	*Not in Vietnam. We're back in this country. You take over universities and break up public property.*
Janice:	*This is no longer the land of opportunity for any except the . . .*

Bob: *No. It is the land of opportunity if you're willing to put forth the effort.*

Janice: *Not true if you're gay, if you're black, or if you're a woman. Not true.*

Bob: *I disagree. I disagree.*

Janice: *. . . an Indian, a Puerto Rican, or a Chicano. It's not true. It's only done for a chosen few . . .*

Bob: *A few token people but those few token people work.*

Janice: *Well then, what is your definition of patriotism?*

Bob: *My patriotism is for my country. I have to identify with something whether it be my country, my region, or something. You have to identify with something.*

Janice: *Why can't you identify with your fellow men and women? I think the changes that have already taken place have actually made you very uncomfortable and that's why we perceive them as changes and you perceive them as setbacks.*

Bob: *What you're saying here is that the country is changing and when enough people change their mind about the war . . .*

Janice: *They have already and nothing's happened.*

Bob: *Why not? If this country has changed . . .*

Janice: *Because it is very lethargic and insensitive to humanitarian ideals and goals and people.*

Bob: *How can we sit and relax, humanitarian and all this, and not maintain defenses? Is every other country in the world going to become humanitarian at the same time? Is Russia, China, Cuba, other countries . . . are they going to sit by idly?*

Janice: *We have to start thinking positively and set examples for them.*

Bob: *O.K. You're saying give up everything. Keep the United States, Alaska, and Hawaii. I presume America is going to be humanitarian and the rest of the world can go their own separate ways.*

Janice: *I would like to work in my country. I'd like to work here. Here is where I have influence. That's what I'd like to work on and I hope the rest of the people all over the world are working on their country for the same kind of goals.*

7.
The New Pluralism

Loyalty to the family in America used to be located on a spectrum somewhere between individualism and patriotism. The traditional progression of values consisted of loyalty to self, to family, and to country. In the last decade, however, all three values were rejected by many Americans who called instead for a higher form of loyalty: to social justice, to humanity, to the planet, to God. And in the first years of this decade there has emerged still another concept of loyalty: the idea of ethnic loyalty, or what has sometimes been described as the New Pluralism.

The debates that rage over these developments are at least to some extent an exercise in semantics. Thus loyalty is now discussed in terms of "identity," and the concept of country has been replaced by the concept of "culture." And perhaps the central question at issue is whether Americans share a common culture with which they can identify—the idea of cultural identity in turn being nothing more perhaps than a sophisticated version of patriotism, or values and perceptions that are held in common by Americans in general.

The standard theory is that America does not have a common culture and that many of its current problems are manifestations of a national identity crisis (*"Who are we?"* as opposed to *"Who am I?"*). Thus the Spanish scholar Enrique Tierno Galván, for example, has said Americans have no shared ideals but simply shared interests rooted in capitalist enterprise. And in this country, Harold Cruse has asserted (sadly) that Marxist class analysis can not be applied to the social problems in America because Marx's theories were based on European societies that had clearly defined national cultures that transcended class structures—societies that could all share "one general cultural communality, the Greco-Christian heritage." Europeans therefore can argue politics without first discussing cultural issues that have already been agreed upon, creating a concept of nationhood and some sense of historical determination. "What is French is a settled question in France, since every Frenchman knows his place in it, and knows how he and his country came to be what they are in modern times." Frenchmen are thus capable of a unified response whenever there is a perceived threat to any of their cultural institutions, such as Coca-Cola's threat to the wine industry.

The cultural stability of other lands can be overstated. Edward T. Hall was discussing this point one sunny afternoon on the patio of his adobe home in Santa Fe, and he said: "There's a problem between northern Italy and southern Italy. They have a problem in Ireland today, a dreadful one. They've always had the problem in England—all these different groups that make up the country—and they don't make any bones about it. And the French have the same kind of thing, and the Germans have it. The only difference in this country has been that we Americans in the past haven't faced up to the problem and admitted it exists."

Our reluctance to do so can be attributed to the idealization of the Melting Pot. But paradoxically, the same country that advocated the homogenization of ethnic groups also has glorified rugged individualism, emphasizing *pluribus* far more than *unum,* the motto on its coins not withstanding. And people who think philosophy creates history, as opposed to expressing it, have traced this individualistic tradition to the ideological influence upon our Founding Fathers of John Locke and his atomistic ontology. Locke said every soul exists in total isolation from all other souls, metaphysically an independent entity that has no organic relationship whatever to the other souls. The soul occupying a body on earth should therefore be allowed as much independence as possible, said Locke, although the souls collectively might enter into a social compact to protect their bodily lives and property. And this resulted in the doctrine that the best government will govern least: in the laissez-faire Jeffersonian democracy that placed the welfare of the individual above the welfare of society.

But the high value placed on individual freedom and initiative can be explained more realistically in terms of the historical necessity for those qualities in the Pilgrim settlers who occupied an alien and hostile shore, and in the pioneers of the Western frontier. It also can be attributed to the social Darwinism that epitomized the early stages of capitalist industrialization in America. Shifting from paradox to irony, however, the contemporary era of postindustrial neo-capitalism has resulted in a repudiation of both individualism and the Melting Pot—on the one hand, a trend toward collectivism or socialization;

on the other hand, the affirmation of a kind of collective individualism represented by the New Pluralism.

But now another paradox arises. In one breath, it is said America has no
common culture. In the next breath, it is said America is in danger of being
totally homogenized by a smothering superculture. And it is fashionable at the
moment to blame this on the domination of the society by White Anglo-
Saxon Protestants—a line of thought that has been developed by the Catholic
scholar Michael Novak and by a number of Jewish intellectuals including
Peter Schrag.

The psychological characteristics of this superculture are said to emphasize
a cold rationality, emotional sterility, the alienation of man from his body and
physical appetites, and the social isolation of the atomistic individual. These
qualities in turn are manifested in a standardized landscape of planned suburbs,
drive-in movies, Howard Johnson restaurants, and McDonald's hamburger
stands; in Disneylands, tasteless frozen food, television programs for the
mentally retarded, and look-alike astronauts whose names nobody remembers.
This is the wasteland created by the Wasp mentality and the logic of the Melting Pot.

Novak and others have responded by calling for a retribalization of white
ethnic groups, the recently-discovered Middle Americans who are primarily
identified with the blue-collar working class. And there is a double motive
involved in this appeal. First, to turn back the tides of the superculture. Second, to prevent a right-wing political coup.

While the new ethnocentrism is often interpreted as a reactionary phenomenon, which it might easily become, it has so far been inspired for the most
part by liberal elements. Indeed, the widespread debate on the subject was
initiated in 1968 by the American Jewish Committee's National Project on
Ethnic America. And the avowed intention has been to organize the ethnics
in their own self-interest before their smoldering resentments are ignited by
racist and neo-fascist demagogues. While the potential political villains may
have been properly identified, however, it is highly questionable that the
Wasps represent the cultural bad guys.

In the first place, it is only recently that the Wasps have been represented
as an ethnic group. Very few Wasps probably think of themselves as ethnics,
and in fact the term Wasp is difficult to define; as political scientist Harold R.
Isaacs has pointed out, there are at least fifty-seven varieties of the species,
and most of them if asked would probably describe themselves simply as
"Americans." That of course is precisely Novak's point—that they represent
the dominant superculture. But that superculture, as it has been described, is
almost certainly a creation not of Wasp ethnicity but of modern technology
and mass production. Its characteristics are those of an advanced industrial
society, and—as economist Kenneth Boulding has proposed—it is becoming

worldwide in scope. It is, said Boulding, the culture of skyscrapers, express-
ways, and airports ("all airports are the same airport"), and it shares both a
common ideology (science) and a common language (technical English).
It has no values as such, other than economic growth, and therefore it threatens
the value systems of countries that do not have an existing culture strong
enough to support it. Thus the Japanese, for example, have been fairly successful in adapting to it; but the superculture as imposed by Mao, on the
other hand, has practically wiped out the previous culture that existed in
China.

In so far as it fails to generate supportive values, it could be argued that the
superculture is not really a culture at all but instead a technological *anti-*
culture. And this raises the question of what we really mean when we refer
to a culture. In most popular definitions, we tend to equate a people's culture
with their literature, art, music, and folk customs—or, at a somewhat deeper
level, with their religions, rituals, and formal philosophies. But these are not
what cultural anthropologists such as Hall mean by culture. These are the
expressions of a culture, or its extensions, and the culture itself is something
else that lies deep below them and provides their foundation or infrastructure.
The culture is what Hall has described as the "hidden dimension." It is a mode
of thought that determines the manner in which an individual perceives reality
and the nature of his relationship to that reality: his relationship to other people, the world, and the universe. According to some linguistic scholars, the
mode of perception called culture is determined to a considerable degree by
language patterns that often reflect radically different conceptions of time,
space, and selfhood. That theory has been contested, but the fact remains
that people in different cultures appear nevertheless to live in different percep-
tual worlds.

Hall himself has pioneered in theories relating to man's use of his environmental space as a specialized function of culture, and it was Hall who coined
the term "proxemics" to describe such theories. Many students know him as
"the space bubble man," referring to his suggestion that all animals including
man have private zones, are surrounded in effect by invisible bubbles of space
they normally prefer to maintain between themselves and their fellow animals.
Crowding, which violates the private zone inside those bubbles, can create
severe emotional stress, upsetting intricate social patterns that are based on
the maintenance of proper spacing; in overpopulated herds, the stress caused
by crowding can actually kill off animals even when there is an abundance of
food available. The same stress presumably affects human beings in our
overpopulated cities and may account for much antisocial behavior, although
to what extent has yet to be learned. "Everybody has a line drawn around
him somewhere," said Hall. But where that line is drawn varies from culture
to culture and from one ethnic group to another. Northern Europeans in

general are more stressed by crowding than are peoples from the Mediterranean area. And Arabs seem to have no bubbles at all; they love to pack in crowds, to rub shoulders and touch each other and bathe in each other's breath while conversing.

All of this is simply to indicate that the subject of ethnicity and cultural differences is far more complicated than is commonly supposed—and especially so since a culture, as defined here, is something that a person has without knowing that he has it. He can not articulate his fundamental perception of reality, even to himself, and such perceptions can not yet be taught in ethnic studies classes. And while there obviously is much to be gained from further study of these perceptions, and while a deeper knowledge and appreciation of them would undoubtedly enrich our society, it remains to be asked if there is anything to be gained at this time in the aggressive assertion of ethnic particularism and the organization of ethnics into self-interest pressure groups.

The New Pluralists clearly are following the pattern of the black cultural nationalists who switched from a politics of protest to a politics of identity, asserting that black is beautiful. That may have been psychologically necessary for some blacks, but it also in many cases has been psychologically damaging, and politically it has proved to be ineffective and even contraproductive. Let us look first at the political aspect and then turn later to the psychological ramifications.

The failure of the American proletariat to develop a unified class consciousness—and therefore, among other possibilities, a viable socialist movement—has been attributed in large part to the persistence of ethnic consciousness in immigrant workers. Thus as Michael Harrington has pointed out, to cite only one example, the southern Italians who came to America at the turn of the century huddled together in the cities and re-established their old village loyalties. "So the Italian workers in the construction industry were hired as crews and were under the control of *padroni*. Their ethnic consciousness thus made it extremely difficult to identify, much less resist, their exploiters, since the middleman with whom they dealt was one of their own countrymen." And as Morris Hillquit observed in 1909, the Socialist Party was "compelled to address the workers of this country in twenty different languages."

Bayard Rustin, in a similar analysis, warned black students that the cultural revolt has been "exclusively preoccupied with racial issues and thus tended to ignore other issues that are also vitally important. . . . you must guard against the possibility of becoming concerned only with intellectual, cultural, and racial issues while the problems of lower- and working-class blacks remain economic." And the Black Panther Party has held that the black cultural nationalism, in Huey Newton's words, "seems to be a reaction instead of a response to political oppression." As the Panthers see it, the social problem is not racism but capitalism.

These views are challenged by Irving Levine, head of the American Jewish Committee's ethnic project. "The failure of what Harrington calls working-class unity," he said, "is based upon the failure of leaders to recognize that differential ethnicity meant differential strategies and tactics. They tried to unify without giving note to particularism, and particularism ended up getting them in the neck. So what we have been saying is that fragmentation takes place in a society not when you pay attention to the fragments but because you don't pay attention to them. You're attempting to create a universal agenda by being abstractly universal. The best way to create a universal agenda is to be directed toward the pieces in a very specific way and build up an agenda from those pieces. By that we mean, pay attention to particularism. Pay attention to the group factor. Pay attention to it in terms of how the people define their group interests, even though they may be wrong occasionally. They may be ethnocentric, chauvinistic, petty-nationalistic. But don't dispense with those feelings and override them with premature universalism, because you'll get backwash. That's my criticism of people I like very much, like Harrington."

But what have been the consequences of black cultural nationalism? The intention of the New Pluralists, as Isaacs expressed it, has been to *depolarize* on social issues and to *repolarize* ethnically. But ethnic polarization in actual practice seems merely to accentuate social polarization, and blacks and whites today are probably more estranged from each other than they have ever been in our recent history. That is certainly true on the campus, where black students have increasingly isolated themselves and white students have become increasingly antagonistic toward the blacks' self-imposed separatism. It also is true in the case of white liberals and radicals who appear to be atoning for their earlier masochism with some tough talk: "I've had it with guilt. The guilt thing doesn't work any more." In short, particularism breeds particularism.

If groups organize in their own self-interest, they can usually succeed only at the expense of some other group. The hardhat used to say: "Equality means the black man gets my job." Now we find the liberal Jew, for example, saying: "Quota hiring means the black man gets *my* job." The groups end up fighting each other for short-term benefits instead of directing their attention collectively to the socio-economic institutions that represent the common source of their difficulties. They fights for slices of a pie instead of storming the bakery or building a better one. The pressure-group tactic of course was refined to a science by Saul Alinsky, who said shortly before his death, "Power has always rested in organization—from the time you had three people in the world, and two of them got together and turned to the third one and said: 'This is the way it's going to be.' " But the third guy probably didn't like that very much, and as a Harvard student put it: "I don't buy the idea of just organizing pressure groups, like Alinsky does, and not caring what they do with their

power. I mean, how would it serve the social interest to organize Scarsdale?"
And we have the example of the Back of the Yards neighborhood in Chicago,
where Alinsky achieved his first major success organizing the white ethnics
who worked in the packinghouses. Back of the Yards is now a conservative
if not a reactionary bastion. And while he said he had no regrets, Alinsky
confessed he did feel a twinge of pain when he revisited the neighborhood and
saw all those cars plastered with Wallace bumperstickers.

As far as psychological rewards go, the assertion of black pride appears
very often to have aggravated the identity crisis it was supposed to resolve.
Black students, for example, are under terrific peer pressure to be just that:
black students. Whether they want to be or not. They can not be English
students or history students or medical students; they must be black students.
And black men are under pressure to be black men, with the emphasis always
on the adjective instead of the noun, the ultimate effect of which can only be
to deny their essential human identity. It also can represent another variation
of the flight from freedom—the sometimes unbearable freedom of individual
autonomy—since it is true, as Isaacs has said, that "a certain lunging back
into the tribal caves is one way to find, maybe, the emotional security that
seems to have disappeared everywhere else." Frantz Fanon went through a
period of mental torment in which he tried to find his identity through what
he called the cosmic Negro myth of a superior black African culture that had
been lost and must be recovered. He "tried to flee myself through my kind . . .
finding Being in Bantu." Transcending that at last, he declared that the
discovery of an ancient black civilization conferred no patent of humanity
upon him. "I am a man," he said, "and in this sense the Peloponnesian War
is as much mine as the invention of the compass. . . . I am a man, and what
I have to recapture is the whole past of the world." He proposed the liberation
of the black man from himself. The black man was no more to be loved than
the Czech, said Fanon, "and truly what is to be done is to set man free."

And yet, Levine was right. And the black cultural nationalists also have
been right. There are cultural differences, and they are important, and they
will continue to frustrate the noble intentions of social reformers and revolutionaries who try to build the New Jerusalem without taking them into account.
The problems of urban renewal, for example, provide an excellent demonstration of this. The city planners move in with blueprints and bulldozers, tear
down an ethnic neighborhood and replace it with one designed to be much
better. They do not recognize that they are destroying complex social systems
that are built into the very physical structure of such neighborhoods—into hall-
ways and corner stores, alleys and vacant lots. They are not aware that some
people need stoops to sit on. And all this is a part of culture, and therefore
unconscious, and the distressed ethnics can not even explain to the planners
what those bulldozers are destroying. This is why Jane Jacobs has insisted

that urban experts can not plan cities that people can live in and that anarchistic development of neighborhoods and cities is much to be preferred; that people should be allowed to build their own cities, piece by piece, as they did in the past, according to their cultural perceptions of what they want and what they need.

The problem is that we do not understand culture. And that in turn is part of the reason we have not yet learned to create social and political institutions that will meet our cultural needs. There are no such institutions existing today anywhere in the industrialized world. Instead there are bureaucracies, and it does not matter whether they are capitalist or socialist. We do not know how to control these bureaucracies and make them respond to our wishes. That is partly because, in a very real sense, we do not consciously know what we want. We do not know what we want because we do not know who we are. We do not understand ourselves; we do not understand culture.

If we do not know enough to plan a decent city, how can we hope to plan a decent society and a decent world? What of those dreams? Levine's criticism to the contrary, social dreamers including Harrington are well aware that the plans they propose "could be welcomed by social engineers and technocrats determined to impose their values on the people" and might simply create another "entrenched bureaucracy with a self-interest of its own." But to this Harrington has added:

"The critics of socialism who cite such dangers ignore, or conceal, the fact that they are the consequence of the complexity of *all forms* of modern technological society and that socialism is the only movement that seeks to make a structural and democratic challenge to the trend. But even more important, it must be understood that there is no institutional reform that, in and of itself, can guarantee genuine popular participation in this process. Only a vibrant movement of the people can do that."

A movement of that nature surely will not be created by a multitude of ethnic pressure groups battling each other in a new version of social Darwinism, each of them asserting and exalting the virtues of a cultural heritage that they themselves do not comprehend. All of our cultures are worth preserving, and the New Pluralism was probably inspired at least in part by a fear that they would be washed out to sea by the trendy tides of the last decade. In that sense, the New Pluralism might be viewed as a conservative movement and an aspect of the neo-orthodoxy that some people have predicted. And all things considered, the Melting Pot was probably a bad idea that should now be discarded. But a perpetual clash of conflicting cultures is not the only alternative, and ethnic awareness need not result in the formation of ethnic pressure groups.

"That would be the modern expectation," said Hall. "As soon as you have a group, it has to be a pressure group. But this is not necessarily the case. We could do something else. And one of the things we could do with ethnicity is to find talents that are available in these groups, and use them creatively. The blacks, for instance, are in general much better at just plain living than most whites. I mean, they know more about having a good time. They know more about being kind and being attentive and about caring for people. And mind you, they also have other things which are dreadfully destructive too. But if we could just begin to see people more for what they are, and what their talents are, and could use them consciously where they go best, in our institutions, then we just might begin to make a little bit of progress."

In other words, we could try to learn from each other. And the New Pluralism in that case might lead to a New Patriotism of shared cultural identities. Not a Melting Pot, but possibly a Mosaic.

8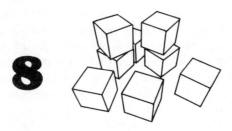

Jerry is an ordained minister who has left the ministry. He tries to explain, by a dramatized encounter, the problems he faced in talking with young people.

Bob:	*You preachers are a gas. You guys are a dying breed as far as I'm concerned. If you're going to survive, you're going to have to be able to justify some purpose in this society. What's your bag? What are you after as a religionist? Why do you have to be a reverend?*
Jerry:	*Maybe that's my need to help people, somehow, regardless of titles or labels. I think maybe I'd like to throw them out. I want to help people to find themselves. I think this is simply the way to live.*
Bob:	*It would be much easier for me to believe that if I didn't know you were a reverend. I wonder, is it a profession?*
Jerry:	*My training is in theology.*
Bob:	*Why don't you resign? It doesn't mean that much to you. You don't like the label.*
Rick:	*I certainly am able to worship within a church but I see Jesus in a much different light than many people see him in the church. I see him as a friend.*
Jerry:	*Are you sitting here telling me, someone that's devoted my entire life to the Church, that you see Jesus Christ more clearly than I do?*
Rick:	*No, listen to what I'm saying. I'm not saying that the Church is out against Jesus. Certainly not. You wouldn't devote your life to Jesus Christ and be against him and I'm sure many thousands of clergy are in love with Jesus as I am. It's a thing that they're not conveying to the people. They're not telling the great gift that God offers . . . the gift of love. The gift of*

love of all people. The gift of being able to love your enemies. They only put it in words. They don't convey it.

Jerry now recounts the day he faced a meeting of his congregation in which he announced that he could no longer serve them.

Jerry: *I've spent seven years with you here in the ministry. We've had a lot of good times and I've certainly appreciated the relationships that we've had. But I really feel that I'm at a point where I can't go any further. I feel that I'm wasting my time at my age. Somewhere, I think I can be more effective with people, to try and help them to find themselves and be more of a whole person. I guess I feel that it isn't here—and where I go, I don't know.*

Bob: *You've been telling us for years that you've got the answer and all of a sudden you come out and say you don't have the answer. What are we supposed to think?*

Jerry: *I don't think I've got all the answers, but . . . I guess I just don't feel that I can be effective here. For a long time, we've had the opportunity to minister to people, to go out and somehow change this world. I think that the Church has still got the stuff to do it with. We've had tons of money that has come our way and what have we done with it? We've spent it on air-conditioning the church. We bought up three houses next door so that we could knock them down and make more parking lots so people didn't have to walk more than a block to church. We've carpeted the sanctuary. We've built rooms. We've bought new tables. We've spent thousands and thousands of dollars on ourselves, and God knows, there are people out there that somehow have got broken lives and they're in a state of need and we're just not meeting it. I tried to talk to you as trustees and you say you agree but when it comes down to the final vote, you vote to buy this property and go ahead and build.*

8.
That Old Time Religion

Religious movements in America during the last decade followed a well-defined pattern that enabled even a casual observer to predict the course of popular theology. First, at any given moment, it was necessary only to determine what had captured the fancy of young people. Shortly afterward that would become the latest fashion in theology, and Harvey Cox would write an article about it for *Playboy*. *Time* magazine would then report this as the newest thing in the New Theology. But the young people meanwhile would have moved on to fresh pastures, the theologians hot on their scent.

It seemed there was nowhere the Now theologians were unprepared to press their pursuit of the Now Generation. They adapted to Hinduism and Zen Buddhism, psychedelic drug mysticism, astrology and witchcraft, political revolution, and cultural revolution. But the young people finally went too far and rediscovered Christian fundamentalism. Unable to accept the Jesus Freaks, the theologians turned in despair to Archie Bunker and the New Pluralism.

But despite its faddish zigging and zagging, the religious revival of recent years has been real and profound. It has occurred for the most part outside the authority of the institutional churches; it has represented, in fact, a reaction against that authority and a repudiation of formal structures that had failed to satisfy man's craving for genuine religious experience. To understand this phenomenon, it is necessary first to review very briefly the history of American theology that led to the Death of God movement in the 1960s.

Liberal Protestant thought in the nineteenth century was deeply influenced by Darwinian theory, resulting in a futuristic and optimistic theology of evolutionary progressivism. Every day in every way, man and the world were becoming better and better. A similar trend in Roman Catholic theology— modernism—was suppressed in 1907 by Pope Pius X, who condemned it as heresy. But the progressivist emphasis in Protestantism continued until faith in man and his worldly works was shattered by World War I and the Great Depression. Humbled for a time, American theologians embraced the neoorthodoxy of Karl Barth: a theology that glorified a starkly transcendent God and scorned man's pride in his petty scientific and technological achievements. But progressivism reasserted itself after World War II, epitomized by Faustian spaceman reaching for the stars and by Faustian theologians who proclaimed the Death of God.

There was nothing pessimistic about the Death of God movement. On the contrary, it was the ultimate expression of optimistic secularism: a celebration of the secular city, the technetronic society, and "a world come of age." It did not mean that God was dead. It meant that God's ultimate essence was a mystery beyond man's understanding, and God wanted man to stop his metaphysical speculations about God's transcendent nature: about that aspect of God that was beyond this world and other than this world. God also was immanent in this world, or of this world, and he wanted man to concentrate on that aspect of God's nature, on "the beyond in our midst." God told theologian Harvey Cox that "the era of metaphysics is dead," that "politics replaces metaphysics as the language of theology," and that "God wants man to be interested not in Him but in his fellow man." God too had heard the Kennedy inaugural. God wanted us to join the civil rights movement and the Peace Corps. He wanted us to march in picket lines, protest injustice, feed the hungry, succor the poor, heal the sick, and comfort the stricken. He also wanted us to stop going to Billy Graham meetings and to stop worrying about eternity and salvation and our precious immortal souls. He wanted us to get involved and to forget all the mumbo-jumbo ritual that took our minds off the problems of this world. Not only was God where it was at. Where it was at *was* God.

In short, the Death of God movement represented theology's all-out effort to make the church "relevant." Especially to the young. But the young, as it turned out, did not respond as expected. The social activists, the heretics, did not need God to give them their marching orders. The nonactivists, the hippies, were looking for another kind of relevance. And secular man in general found little to inspire him in the new jazzed-up version of the social Gospel. As Andrew M. Greeley put it:

"The typical divinity school graduate went through a hell of a time with his own religious problems and his exposure to the New Theology and the emphasis on relevance and all. He came out pretty much convinced that modern man, whoever that is, was no longer religious. And then he went out to his parish and thought he was dealing with modern man. And he wasn't. He was dealing with people who still had obvious and explicit religious needs—to which he did not address himself. He talked politics, he talked social action, he talked culture. He didn't talk religion. Well, you can get politics-social action-culture from anybody, and most of them people who are more sophisticated than your pastor. What you want from him is religion. Now, there may be ethical consequences to religion. Fine. But let them be defined as consequences and not as substitutes. Contemporary man needs religion as much as his caveman ancestors did, if not more, and for the same basic reason: he needs something to believe in, some answers to the fundamental questions about life and death."

There are problems and mysteries. When the social problems have all been solved, the mysteries will remain. And then the mysteries themselves will become problems—as indeed, in many cases, they already are. Men fear death, loneliness, and boredom. They fear them now, and they will fear them all the more in the future, in a postscarcity world, after the abolition of compulsory labor, when the Kingdom of Necessity is replaced by the Kingdom of Freedom. Freedom to do what? And for what purpose? Such a social utopia could be a spiritual hell.

As we have seen, middle-class young people during the affluent 1960s lived for a time in what might be considered a prototypal Kingdom of Freedom. For many of them, it was a hell. Some of them put off consideration of the mysteries and involved themselves in social activism, as adults will often involve themselves in work. But others sought for answers to those fundamental questions, and in doing so they turned in many cases to Asia and to drugs.

They turned in other words to religion and mysticism. And it was no accident that found them facing East instead of West. Western science and rationalism appeared at least to have destroyed the traditional foundations of religious belief, putting nothing in their place, and Western theology was not interested at the moment in doing anything to restore or reaffirm them. A vacuum had been created, and the almost inevitable result was the Leap to the East. In Eastern metaphysics and mystical experience, one still found answers to death, loneliness, and boredom. And psychedelic drugs seemed to have a capacity to produce such an experience: a direct and immediate experience of God or Ultimate Reality or whatever you preferred to call it. At the very least, they most definitely did have the capacity to enhance sensory perceptions—and this in itself made them highly attractive to young people, for reasons touched on by Edward T. Hall during that conversation on his patio in the warm New Mexican sunlight. Looking out at a distant mountain range, he said:

"Talk about crowding and what's happening to our cities. We haven't taken this seriously, but the population of the United States has doubled since I was born. And when I was born, over half the population was living in the country, and now it's something like a fifth of the population is living in the country, and all the rest of it is living in the cities. And all these people eat more. Their standard of living has gone up, and they consume more. So that puts pressure on the production of beef and chickens and vegetables and everything else. So what we've done is turn the United States into a factory. And you get techniques for producing beef, for example, where you force-feed the animals and fill them up with hormones, to get them to market quicker. You can no longer afford to produce meat which has any flavor, and nothing has any flavor any more.

"Now, what does it do to a population when nothing tastes any good? Eating is one of the most basic things people do. And when you remove the flavor from all the food, you have done something. Of course nobody designed it that way, and it isn't any plan; it could happen to the Communists just as easily as it happened to us, and it's not capitalism that did it. It's something else. But when you begin to downgrade the senses, and you overload the cities with smoke and smog and terrible smells, then everybody lives a miserable life no matter how much money he has.

"You buy something, and it's not well-made. It falls apart. It doesn't feel good. It doesn't smell good. It doesn't sound good. And it doesn't taste good. So we've created an environment—again, without design—that's been working on people in very subtle, continuous ways, degrading life. And there aren't any satisfactions.

"Watching television, for example, is a very bad thing if you watch too much of it, and most people do. Because what stimulation do you get out of a television set? And there aren't any places for kids to play and get exercise— they grow up in apartments, many of them—and there are lots of studies now that indicate you can actually stunt their intellectual development and make idiots out of them if they don't develop muscular skills and co-ordination in the process of growing up. So they're mentally deprived, and they're bored, because everything that has happened to them has been phony.

"But it's been phony in such subtle ways that they don't know what it is. They don't know what's wrong. All they know is, something's wrong. They've eaten a lot of meat that doesn't taste like anything, and they've consumed a lot of products that are poorly made. And they don't know any better, because how could they know that meat was supposed to taste any different? And their senses have been assaulted in all sorts of ways.

"Another thing—a very insidious thing—is the breaking of everything. I mean, nothing is ever completed in this country. You take school bells, for example. As soon as you get started and get into something, the damn bell rings. And that fragments life, so the kid learns very early that you break life up and artificially segment it. It's the same on television, with the commercials. Nothing has any continuity to it. There's no country in the world that interrupts people like we do. And what happens if you start something and then you can't complete it? This makes a particular kind of imprint on the nervous system, and it has a particularly insidious effect upon people when they never finish anything.

"So the kids know something's wrong, and they react. But since they don't know what's wrong, they pick the strangest things to react against; like inhibitions on swearing, or marriage, or the family. Stuff like that."

All of which may go a long way toward explaining youth's antagonism to the accumulation of material possessions—most of it junk—and also the vague but persistent demand for "authenticity." It certainly helps to explain the attraction of psychedelic drugs, which can make *everything*—including junk—look, smell, feel, taste, and sound very good. So the young people with their jaded senses would drop acid, and they would look at the world, and they would see that it was very good.

At a deeper level, however, the drug experience also had a capacity to stop clocks. Nothing segments life more than the ticking of clocks, every tick marking the passage of a quantum of time, and the mystic does not experience time at all. He experiences eternity. And eternity in this sense is not to be confused with endless time. It is outside of time. The mystic lives wholly in the here-now present moment, where past and future come together, and he understands that time itself is an illusion, that ultimate reality is eternal, and that life in consequence is also eternal and therefore immortal. *He* is immortal. There is no death. There is only life everlasting, outside of time, which always was and always will be. Moreover, the mystic is supremely content to live in that here-now present moment, without regrets or expectations, since of course there is no real past to regret or future to anticipate. There is nothing new under the eternal sun; but the serene mystic does not require the stimulus of novelty, and therefore he is never bored, he simply *is*. He is content to be, and he is not concerned with becoming.

Nor does he suffer the loneliness and alienation of atomized autonomy. Because in fact he is one with the universe and other people, and the self that he is does not end at his fingertips. While he loses his sense of individual selfhood, in doing so he gains the world; in losing himself he finds himself. He discovers the universal Self that is nothing less than pure Being. There is no Other. There is only the One, and he is that One.

So drug mysticism offered young people a way to achieve personal salvation. It remains to be asked what, if any, are the social consequences of this kind of religion.

One aspect of mysticism that we have referred to here suggests that there are no such consequences. In so far as it denies the reality of time, mysticism also denies the reality of history and progress—and therefore, in consequence, the necessity for social struggle to create a better world. In rejecting the dualism of past and future, mysticism also tends to reject all other dualisms—including the dualism of good and evil. The world is just fine as it is, and the problem is simply that the rational mind deceives people and make it impossible for most of them to recognize that everything is really All Right. As we said earlier, hippies did believe that mass changes of individual consciousness would ultimately result in social salvation; the entire population eventually would be turned on by drugs and thus would find peace. But the concept that consciousness precedes structure does nevertheless contribute to social quietism.

Mystical ontology on the other hand could tend to encourage social activism. We have discussed Galbraith's thesis that the private sector in America is reluctant to deal with the social needs that exist in the public sector, and this reluctance can be traced to our cultural perception of a society that consists of atomized individuals who have no organic relationship to one another. In his classic study, *The Meeting of East and West,* philosopher F.S.C. Northrop wrote: "Consciously or unconsciously, the Lockean doctrine of the self-sufficient, independent, moral, religious, and political person has become so much a common-sense assumption of the vast majority that in a political showroom, when emotions are raised and traditional, instinctive reactions are released, the laissez-faire, individualistic response triumphs over the organic, social principle." As we have seen, however, individuals in mystical ontology are not atoms at all. There is a cosmic connection that relates each to the other; they share a common essence in which each in fact *is* the other. And to the extent that the mystic feels related to others, he will presumably care about the welfare of others. "When you're cut, I bleed. I should see to it, therefore, that you are not cut."

It should be emphasized at this point that we have been talking here about Eastern mysticism—and that the West too has a mystical tradition. And while there are many similarities between the two traditions, there also are important differences. Thus the Western mystic may also experience the timelessness of eternity, for example, but Western theology does not regard mundane history as an illusion. Rather, it is a process that will culminate in the Last Days, when history will end and mankind will enter the eternal Kingdom of God. The mystic is permitted a vision of this kingdom, but the true end of time has not yet occurred.

Eastern mysticism in addition tends to be pantheistic, suggesting that God is nothing more than the totality of all the little selves that actually are one Self. The West insists that God transcends man—that he is something *more* than man—although man and God are intimately connected in what Martin

Buber has called an I-Thou relationship. The West also insists on the integrity of the individual selves or souls, although it does not propose they are isolated atoms; they too are united in an I-Thou relationship. And that hyphen that connects them is love, which is an attraction that can exist only between selves that are not the same Self. And God is love.

Western mysticism perhaps is less vulnerable to quietism, and more likely to have social consequences, in as much as it suggests that the Kingdom of God is not a nirvana that already exists. The kindom is an Omega Point that lies in the future and must be achieved—through the efforts of men, with the grace of God—and indeed the Theology of Hope has proposed in this sense that God is neither dead nor alive; rather, he is Not-Yet. He is the God who will be, at the end of the evolutionary process, with the collective salvation of man. Such a concept obviously does have social consequences, and, significantly, its development by European theologians was inspired by the theories of a Marxist-atheist, the German philosopher Ernst Bloch.

Drug mysticism in this country during the 1960s was more Eastern than Western. But that may have been due to the fact that the emergence of the drug subculture coincided with the intellectual Leap to the East and the widespread interest in Eastern metaphysical literature. There also was an Eastern bias on the part of the drug movement's gurus—Aldous Huxley, Timothy Leary, and Alan W. Watts. Expectation plays a major role in the nature of a psychedelic drug experience, and most of the people who originally dropped acid were anticipating an Eastern religious experience. Which is not to say that all of them had such an experience, or that everybody who took drugs was searching for religious insights. And with the passage of time, the drug movement in general degenerated from a search for God to a search for kicks.

LSD and other hard psychedelics are rarely used in a strictly religious context these days, and most people turn on simply to blow their minds and enjoy the pretty lights. Many minds have been permanently exploded, and it is not news that drugs have become a very bad scene. There is reason for serious concern about increased drug use in high schools and in factories; however, it is my own impression that the abuse of drugs on campus peaked in 1970-71, declined sharply during the 1971-72 academic year, and in fact is not at the moment a major problem at the college level. Touring the country, I found virtually no heroin on campus, and very little tripping with LSD and other hard psychedelics. Amphetamines were used, but for an old-fashioned purpose—to cram for exams. Marijuana was commonplace, but it was used for the most part like cocktails, to relax after work. Alcohol had made a comeback and was used in a similar fashion. And as suggested previously, this may be due in part to the Little Brother effect. If political radicalism during the late 1960s spread to the high schools, where students worked it out of their systems before they entered college, the same could be said of drug abuse.

"I went through the whole thing during my junior year in high school," said a freshman coed at Iowa Wesleyan College. "All my friends were just getting into it then—the whole works, even shooting up—and of course it was a big deal to smoke dope. There was a lot of peer pressure to do it, and I did it all. So now I've done it, and I'm burned out. I have no desire to do it any more."

"There's a lot of folk knowledge about drugs now," said an English major at Harvard. "Students didn't believe all that medical scare talk, but now we've got a generation of users we can look at and see the effects with our own eyes. You can look at a guy who had it all together, you thought, and now he's maybe dead or in a psycho ward. And we've got a lot of street people in Cambridge, and you look at some of these kids fourteen years old strung out on drugs asking you for a dime, and you say: 'Well, this isn't what I want.' "

"Dope is way down this year," said a sophomore co-ed at Oberlin College. "Last year there was still a lot of acid and just an incredible amount of tripping —especially around exam times. People would do it in the middle of the week. So who cared about tests and classes? And I had friends missing two weeks of class, and their grades took a downward plunge. But this year there's almost no acid around. There's no cocaine on campus, and no needle freaks, and people are really concentrating on their studies—just drowning them-selves in liberal arts. There's a lot more liquor consumption. And there's still a lot of grass. But that's mostly brought in by the freshmen—to bowl over the upperclassmen, so they think. And at Oberlin it's usually used now to deal with the Friday night identity crisis. You know, because it's the end of the week and the end of classes, and you're supposed to freak out and say: 'Who am I?' And this ties into another thing—the ecology stuff and the whole health food business. People are really concerned now what they put in their bodies, including a lot of chemicals."

"There was a time when a significant number of people were doing a lot of acid here," said a University of Chicago philosophy senior. "But the con-sequences of that were to show their friends it's not a useful thing to do; that it can't be a permanent way of life. Now there's a lot of alcohol, and there's a lot of grass, but they're used pretty strictly in a recreational way. Like you've just finished something, and now this is the time just to flop on the bed and just sit there and listen to the stereo and have a good time. And another thing is, I don't think now you have the peer-group pressure you might have had a few years ago. If you smoke dope, you're not impressing anybody. And no-body cares if you don't smoke it."

"It's that way with me," said the Harvard student. "A surprising number of people find that grass just isn't that pleasant. Not as pleasant as alcohol, for instance. And my own experience leads me to believe this. I mean, you take the very things grass was lauded for in the early days: that it upset your perception of things, amplified your self-doubts, made you re-evaluate your life. I think it probably does that for some people. And that kind of upset isn't always comfortable or helpful for a person."

"People react so differently to grass," said the Oberlin coed. "I know some people whose minds just actually explode, and they can write papers and work very well when they're on grass. But the majority of kids get catatonic or very sleepy or just very buzzed out, and they enjoy things differently. They think of little funny things to do, like building toothpick castles and stuff. But that's not exactly a very constructive way to spend your time—especially when the pressure's on to compete for grades. And that competition now is just fantastic."

A further insight was offered by Philip Seitz, a Chicago analyst who has in the past treated many young people with drug-related emotional problems. "As everybody knows," he said, "hippies are much fewer in number now. I used to see lots of them, but not any more. The peak was a few years ago, and since then it's been tapering off. I'm not sure why. But I do know that every hippie I treated sooner or later gave up all drugs as a bad scene that didn't answer his problems. And I think it's significant that I've seldom treated a younger child in a family who had seen the destruction drugs did to an older brother or sister he had previously admired. I also found hippies over a period of time tended to evolve toward the Yippie philosophy. And I think that had to do with their drug patterns. They'd start with mild drugs like pot, which got them introverted and rather depressed. And during that phase they were flower children. But then they'd get into speed, into amphetamines, and that made them very irritable, aggressive, and hostile. I saw this metamorphosis of hippie into Yippie many times. It gradually changes a person's personality from depressive and introverted to more aggressive and paranoid."

In fact a recent study by psychiatrist Solomon H. Snyder suggests that speed can produce what appears to be a classic model of paranoid schizophrenia. And for what it's worth, a former SDS member told me he remembers keeping himself high on speed to stay awake during the Weatherman Days of Rage in Chicago in 1969. But the use of drugs was never popular with militant activists, who take the position that opiates are the opiate of the people. Which accounts for the schism between Eldridge Cleaver, the exiled Black Panther Party information minister, and Timothy Leary, the exiled LSD shaman. As social critic Leslie Fiedler has said, Cleaver speaks of Leary with the same distaste the Chamber of Commerce does.

I do not mean to imply that the decline in drug mysticism has meant a decline in religious enthusiasm and the search for religious meaning by a significant proportion of the youth population. That continues. And the New Theology until recently at least has tried to keep up with it. When it became obvious the young people were not interested in their Death of God brand of secular relevance, the with-it theologians decided it was time for theology to move "beyond the secular" in a series of adaptive contortions it would be too tedious and pointless to describe in this limited space. They even attempted to romance the heretics, constructing revolutionary theologies that suggested God wanted us to occupy administration buildings and destroy the military-industrial conspiracy. But the avant garde could not stomach the Jesus Freaks, as noted, and the last time I checked they were trying to relate theology to the ethnic pluralism discussed in the previous chapter. As for the new crop of seminarians now coming up, many of them appear to have lost their enthusiasm for copycat social relevance.

"Faculties today almost have to push students," said the University of Chicago church historian Martin E. Marty. "For example, I read the history papers of our nine new students. Three years ago, those papers would all have been the up-against-the-wall kind of thing. This year, on eight of the nine, I had to write: 'Don't forget—Christian ministry *does* have a social dimension.' I don't mean these people are buying the system. But they realize, I think, that things aren't quite so simple, and our problems today are much more complicated than we thought, and they're looking for new ways to really be effective."

As for the Jesus Freaks, he said: "I don't invest a lot of hope in any of the specific forms of organization they take. In a media-oriented society, they'll distintegrate very fast. But I believe they're part of a larger thing that has been around for a long time and is going to keep being around. And that's the quest for immediate experience. My generation was taught to accept the mediated experience, and I'm perfectly content with it. But the Jesus Freaks and the Catholic Pentecostal kids are really telling us you can't go on for another generation talking about the fact that once upon a time people had experiences. Which is what mainline religion always says. And we have to get back to the point of being allowed to have our own experiences. At the same time, as I said, there's also a little more willingness to deal with complexity. I think they're all finding that in a complex world the immediate experience very often forces them to reflect. They've found you can't just stay in ecstasy. At the same moment that you're grasping for new experience, you're also pressured into being a little more willing to reflect on it. And the Jesus movement as such—I think some of it will denominationalize, and when it's finished there'll be a couple of new little Jesus sects. That's how Americans do things. Others will disappear, like the student radicals, and blend back into society. But I think the majority of them will take something of it back to the mainline churches."

It is not surprising that the only institutional churches that are flourishing today are the fundamentalist churches—the churches that Robert Coles has written so movingly about, where sharecroppers and migrant workers sing and pray and speak in tongues to their God and ask him for the strength and the understanding to bear their burdens and face their fears. (*"I come out of there and I'm taller,"* said a tenant farmer in North Carolina. *"I'm feeling bigger. I feel God has taken me to Him. He put his hand on my shoulder . . ."*)

I was reading William James. And he said that religion consists in "the belief that there is an unseen order, and that our supreme good lies in harmoniously adjusting ourselves thereto."

I was talking to Andrew Greeley about the Jesus Freaks. I told him they seemed to have a curious quality that had somehow impressed me—something in their faces, a kind of joyful radiance I did not understand. And he said:

"Oh, it's faith, you know. It's not a sophisticated faith. But it's faith. Those people believe in something."

I was reading Teilhard de Chardin, and he said:

"Nothing is more mistaken than the view that religion is a primitive and transitory stage through which mankind passed in its infancy. The more man becomes man, the more will it be necessary for him to be able to, and to know how to, worship."

9

A group of students and teachers meet together. Gerry, acting as guide, passes the discussion from teachers to students and back to teachers.

Gerry: *What would you say most of the teaching in the school system is today?*

Rachel: *I can only talk about the one I'm familiar with and I think that we are trying both systems, free classroom and traditional classroom. We have experiments going on where you have the free system, you do as you want to.*

Bonnie: *I would feel comfortable making the generalization that for the most part public education in this country is authoritarian, too structured, dehumanizing, brutalizing, and knocks natural creativity out of kids. It teaches them how to form, how to follow patterns, teaches them not to ask why, teaches them to accept blindly the kinds of things they are told by authority figures and the kinds of things they read in print.*

Paul: *In reading about educational systems all over the country, there are changes that are coming about . . .*

Bonnie: *Too late! And too slow . . .*

Rachel: *If it's too late we might as well give up and not do anything.*

Gerry: *Now, you've heard a lot of what the teachers have said. Why don't we ask the students?*

Jimmy: *School takes our creativity, that's true. It's almost like being conditioned. You go to class when the bell rings. You leave when the bell rings. You have to do everything by the rules, by the book, nothing you do on your own can get you out of school. You're taught to be a data processing machine. They feed you data and you feed back your work.*

George: *I don't like the idea of being a machine and I would agree*

	with him. Like teaching today is more like 'follow the leader' because it's like you were doing exercises. If I had my way, I would ask the students what they want to be in life and I would teach them everything in that direction.
Susan:	*Believe it or not, we are the leaders of tomorrow. I think it's about time we were taken seriously and encouraged and told that's okay, because we know that our world is going to be different.*
Emily:	*In school you have all the grading, which is, as I see it, to force people to compete with each other . . . to make them be alone, not develop communities among themselves because you're always supposed to do better work than anybody else. I think that's backfiring. I think most of the people who are in the schools now are wise to the fact that you're not really learning anything. You might as well help each other get through it.*
Susan:	*Sometimes a student can relate better to another student and a teacher can't explain as well as it can be explained by someone on your own level. So what's wrong with having a classroom where the seats are pushed closer together and you work together on something. When people are working together I think that's better. They can be individuals together.*
Gerry:	*What would you particularly like to see the school become? Adults, do you have any suggestions?*
Bonnie:	*I would like to see the students be able to be creative and realize their good and bad points and for them to be individuals and to enjoy that.*
Rachel:	*I would like to see a school where students left it and still wanted to learn and knew how to learn, with or without school.*
Joe:	*I think a school where a student can be given direction to enjoy life, to know that life has to be enjoyed as an individual and yet as part of a whole.*
Harry:	*I'd like to see fewer students per teacher.*
Lois:	*I think students should be taken seriously and as real people because they are.*
Joe:	*Students should be made aware that the schools have shortcomings but these shortcomings are really the shortcomings of society and education is being faulted as a profession for the people who are to solve all of society's problems today, without exception.*

9.
No More Pencils, No More Chalk

To the extent that the political and cultural protests of the last decade were made possible by an extension of education, it is not surprising that the educational institution itself became not only a base for radical activity but also a prime target of radical criticism. And this criticism took many forms. It was frequently argued, for example, that education at all levels must be made "relevant." But while some critics called for a return to traditional values of teaching and scholarship, others called for the abolition of compulsory education—the deschooling of America.

At the university level, relevance was defined to imply a pertinence to the political Revolution. Shakespeare was thus irrelevant because he did not address himself to the problems of economic and social injustice in capitalist society, and high culture in general was irrelevant for the same reason; as one student said: "It has nothing to do with the fact that rats are biting babies in the slums of Chicago." In the ghetto, in turn, relevance was defined—by people who didn't live there—in terms of educational content and techniques that related directly to the everyday life and the supposed survival needs of the children who do live there.

On the campus, at least, relevance is no longer a magic word. With the failure of the Movement, students were at liberty to pursue their own interests and ambitions—what was relevant to them as individuals. And they have been doing just that, concentrating on their studies and outside activities and personal emotional needs. As a student editor at Harvard said: "The editor of the *Crimson* at one point said he could no longer study medieval poetry because it did not relate to the war in Vietnam. Which is just ridiculous. I think students now generally feel something is relevant because it is good, the best of what is known as thought in the world, and that's relevant enough." Another Harvard student who was a campaign worker during the 1972 primaries added: "The world isn't all politics. It's also art and English history." And an Oberlin coed said: "Relevant was such an overused word that people fell back on. It became such an all-out excuse if you didn't like something: 'Well, that's not relevant.' And then you didn't have to explain it, of course. And the only people who use that now are the black kids that we take in from the slum areas who can't spell and can't write a good composition. You know, we're filling up our quota. And they'll sit in class and won't say anything, or if you ask them a direct question they'll just say: 'That's not relevant.' This has happened so often, and one of the white kids in my sociology class blew his top and said: 'I finally figured out what that means. It means you don't understand it or you don't know how to do it.' And it's a bunch of shit."

That comment will be discussed later. But as the educator Joseph J. Schwab told his University of Chicago students at the peak of the radical period, the purpose of feeding hungry people is not just to have them fed. The ideal is not people with full stomachs and empty heads. There also is beauty and wisdom in the world, and it has been a function of the university to preserve and nourish those values, so they will be there for all people when the people have the hands to pick them up. And as Kevin Starr has complained, there is still an academic hangover from the relevant 1960s in terms of sloppy work, suggesting that one of the major challenges of the 1970s will be to regain some sense of relation to high culture. The counterculture, for example, certainly failed to contribute anything to that tradition—no literature, no art, no music that will survive. We had a lost generation before, in the 1920s; but it did not sever its ties to the West's cultural heritage, and it produced as its spokesman an F. Scott Fitzgerald. This time around, we had to settle for Abbie Hoffman. Pop art had its own values, which we will look at in the next chapter, but I do find it very hard to avoid a personal preference for Fitzgerald.

Having rejected relevance, students also have abandoned the idea of seizing control of the universities and using them as a power base to revolutionize the structure of society. "I used to think you could accomplish significant things on a broad scale by doing things within the university," said the student campaign worker quoted earlier. "I thought that somehow if you changed Harvard, you would be able to change the larger society. Well, it's important to change Harvard. But that's not really what I want to do, and that's probably why I got into presidential politics. I want something bigger than Harvard University."

This does not mean students and other critics are content with the existing university system; and indeed attacks upon that system have come from both the right and left—the charge in each case being that the standards of teaching and scholarship have been allowed to deteriorate. Spiro T. Agnew thus charged from the right that universities "have lost sight of the traditional, time-honored purpose of education," and he urged them to "restore the ivory tower and the classical education that has been the bedrock of our civilization." And essentially the same indictment is heard from the left; the quality of teaching has declined, students do not receive well-rounded liberal educations, and the university is no longer a community of scholars dedicated to the intellectual adventure and the advancement of knowledge. But Agnew attributed this state of affairs to educational permissiveness and an emphasis on relevance: "this modern trend of yielding to student demands for courses that concern themselves with the major political and social issues of the day." The left on the other hand has blamed it on an "industrialization" of higher education that has turned the university into a "knowledge factory" designed to train technocrats and to meet the research and development needs of corporations and the government (in particular, the Pentagon).

But still another point of view has been proposed by Bruno Bettelheim, who said: "I think if a considerable majority of students say this university, while it meets some of their needs, is very uncomfortable for them, I think they are right. If they say higher education is in need of radical reformation, I think they are right. I think it is unnatural to keep a young person for some twenty years in dependency. Or in school. I think this is unnatural. I think this might be a way of life for a small elite which always in the past went to universities. There were those who could go to school for twenty years. But they were never more than a small percentage of the population. Now we have the tremendous push that everybody should go to college. It has brought an incredibly large number of kids into the university who do *not* find their self-realization through study, or the intellectual adventure."

In other words, as we indicated in Chapter Three, the deterioration of academic standards and the depersonalization of higher education were due in large part to the massive enrollments resulting from affluence and the postwar baby boom. This is not to say the left has not been correct in asserting that the alliance of education with the military-industrial complex has degraded traditional values of education; that criticism is perfectly valid. But Bettelheim perhaps has identified an even more fundamental problem: that universities are crowded with an unprecedented number of students, and that many of these students do not really want to be on campus. Even if those traditional values of higher education were preserved or restored, there are undoubtedly millions of young people who would not find them compatible with their real interests, ambitions, and needs. The Carnegie Commission on

Higher Education estimated in 1972 that 5 to 15 per cent of the nation's college and university students were "reluctant attenders" who enrolled mainly because of social or parental pressures. And the actual percentage is probably much higher. While more than 90 per cent of Daniel Offer's modal adolescents planned to attend college, for example, only 4 percent indicated that reading or studying was the activity they most enjoyed. The university to some extent might be restructured to adapt to the needs of the youthful majority, and indeed the protests of the 1960s did produce some worthwhile reforms. But as Bettelheim has said, such reforms can be carried to a point where the university loses its character as an institution dedicated to the intellectual virtues and the frontiers of knowledge. "It becomes a therapeutic institution which really is asked to do an impossible task: namely, to meet the needs of an adolescent age group in ways that they can not be met."

This reality inspired the late Paul Goodman to reject the idea of student power and to suggest that its advocates instead might be better advised not to enter college. Goodman in fact recommended a drastic reduction of schooling in general, including the elimination of most high schools, and a new emphasis on apprenticeship and other forms of incidental education. "Our aim should be to multiply the path of growing up, with opportunity to start again, cross over, take a moratorium, travel, work on one's own." Persons so inclined could still enter universities, of course, and the universities for their part would be "better off unencumbered by sullen, uninterested bodies."

But the most radical and controversial critic of the educational system has been Ivan Illich, who resigned from the Roman Catholic priesthood to direct the Center for Intercultural Documentation, a free university he founded in Cuernavaca, Mexico. Illich has called for nothing less than the total abolition of compulsory education at all levels and the replacement of schools with a variety of innovative systems that would allow children and adults to cultivate their own interests. The government would issue all citizens credit cards that would permit them to utilize educational services ranging from personalized tutoring by skill teachers to a computerized dating operation that would put people in touch with other laymen who share their intellectual interests.

Essential to Illich's philosophy is the idea that people learn best from everyday life, as opposed to the abstract theories about life that are taught in the classrooms; he believes that natural curiosity is the best incentive for intellectual development, allowing a person "to learn what he wants to know," and that "enforced instruction deadens the will for independent learning in most people."

Another prominent spokesman for such views has been Everett Reimer, whose advocacy of them before a seminar audience inspired Edgar Friedenberg to remark that abolition of obligatory schooling "is as unlikely as the abolition of prostitution." Friedenberg added: "Any institution in which so many people can count on getting screwed is not going to be abolished by a mandate of the people; especially by a mandate of the American people."

B. F. Skinner and Jonathan Kozol, among others, have offered a more thoughtful (if less colorful) rebuttal of Illich's basic premise. Discussing this over a beer one night, Skinner said:

"I'm opposed to the use of extensive punishment—it's not necessary—but I'm not in favor of permissiveness either. I'm not in favor of letting the kids do what they want to do. Because they don't want to do the things that are going to be important for them to learn. And that's a misake that's been made for two hundred years, that goes back to Rousseau: to let kids learn as they learn in the world at large. But you can't do that, because what they're going to be learning in school isn't something which at the moment is interesting to them. It's impossible. Now, you can set up reward systems—or what we call contingencies of reinforcement—that can make the students very much interested in what you really want them to do, which is learn something. But you can't bring the future into the classroom. And I think millions of kids are being sacrified today on the altar of educational theories, and it's just a tragic thing and very hard to change."

Skinner has written that it is possible in education to use his system of rewards, or positive reinforcers, to "bring about the changes in the student we want to bring about." But who are the *"we"* he is talking about, and what specifically are these changes that *"we"* want to bring about? There also is a danger here, which Skinner himself has acknowledged, that reward systems might control behavior to a point where any opposition to the controls would become virtually impossible. "When people are being pushed around, controlled by methods which are obvious to them, they know who and what is controlling them, and when things become too aversive, they turn against the controller." But the use of rewards might make it difficult to identify the source of the control. "Even though you are inclined to revolt, you don't know whom to revolt against."

But there is at least one thing almost everybody would agree that *"we"* want students to do, which is to learn how to read. And it is significant that the most devastating criticism of the failure of free schools to teach reading has come from Jonathan Kozol, author of *Death at an Early Age* and a pioneer himself in the free school movement.

Noting that the average life of a free school has been nine months, Kozol wrote in *Psychology Today* that "the major cause for failure in the free schools is our unwillingness or inability to teach the hard skills." While some children can learn to read by themselves, the same way they learn to talk, in most cases "it is both possible and necessary to teach reading in a highly conscious, purposeful, and sequential manner." Kozol said he still believed education should be individualized, unoppressive, and open-structured. "There *is* a question, however, about the naive, noncritical acceptance of the unexamined notion that you can not *teach* anything. It is just not true that the best teacher is the grownup who most successfully pretends that he knows nothing or has nothing to suggest to children." Kozol attacked in particular the notion that children will ask how to read when they want to learn how, since that time seems never to arrive. And the urban free schools do not go out of business because of pressure from public officials; they collapse because the parents of the black and Spanish-speaking pupils take their children out of the schools, and the parents do that because they want their children to read. They do not want them to "make clay vases, weave Indian headbands, play with Polaroid cameras, and climb over geodesic domes." They want their children to have the same skills the college-educated teachers both scorn and possess. They are not interested in the white-oriented counterculture and teachers who tell them their children "do not need college, do not need money, do not need ugly, contaminated, wicked, middle-class success." And the reason is elementary. "The issue for these children is not success. It is survival." Which led Kozol to conclude that "Harlem does not need a new generation of radical basket-weavers. It does need radical, strong, subversive, steadfast, skeptical, rage-minded, and power-wielding obstetricians, pediatricians, lab technicians, defense attorneys, building-code examiners, brain surgeons."

A similar analysis can be applied to the failure of the experimental and highly-publicized Ocean Hill-Brownsville Demonstration District school project conducted during 1967-70 in New York City. The idea there was to upgrade ghetto education through community control of the schools and through innovative teaching programs that included self-programmed reading materials, a Montessori-style kindergarten, and an Afro-American Studies Center. And it did not work. The situation was complicated by conflict with the Board of Education bureaucracy and the United Federation of Teachers, who viewed the project as a threat to their own entrenched positions. The fact remains, however, that the eight schools in the district had a high rate of absenteeism—perhaps as high as 70 per cent in some cases—and that reading scores did not improve. On the contrary, they declined. At the end of the experiment, the children in the district were actually poorer readers than they had been before. And again, the parents of the children were not impressed by the assertion of academic reformers that reading scores merely reflected the biased values of white middle-class culture and that their youngsters were receiving a far richer and more humanistic education. The parents wanted academic improvement that would allow their children to enter the middle class. Political philosopher Diane Ravitch summed up the situation: "Schools exist, in the first instance, to provide basic literacy. Schools which can not teach reading and writing can not teaching anything else, certainly not humane values. It may be that standardized achievement tests elicit the 'wrong kind' of learning, whatever that means, yet parents generally expect the schools to deliver literacy before embarking on innovative paths."

And what about those black college students who annoyed that Oberlin coed because they couldn't read or write and interpreted all "white" education as irrelevant? The antagonism that provoked no doubt was inspired to a considerable extent by the fact that higher education has recently become easily accessible only to the very rich and to the very poor who enter on scholarship programs. And the mass of students, caught in the middle by the financial pinch, resent the "ingratitude" of the black scholarship students. But what if the blacks do use "irrelevant" to describe information they do not understand, that is alien to their life experience and therefore devoid of any meaning or content? Isn't that what irrelevance really amounts to? And isn't the real tragedy the fact that so much of the West's wisdom and culture indeed are, in the literal sense, irrelevant to these people? Speaking to this issue, Bayard Rustin said: "Everyone knows that education for the Negro is inferior. Bring them to the university with the understanding that they must have remedial work they require. The easy way out is to let them have black courses and their own dormitories and give them degrees. . . . What in hell are soul courses worth in the real world? No one gives a damn if you've taken soul courses. They want to know if you can do mathematics and write a correct sentence."

There clearly is a difference between academic relevance or freedom and academic anarchy. A. S. Neill founded the Summerhill school in England, which advocated freedom and innovation in educational practice, and there was subsequently a Summerhill movement in America. And when Neill came to America, I was told by Bettelheim, he said: "All my life I have preached freedom. And what my American followers make out of it is chaos."

In this context, it is important to identify the fundamental social assumptions that are inherent in the concept of deschooling. Consider, for example, Illich's criticisms of "knowledge capitalism" and an educational system that "serves the dominant minority as a justification for the privileges they claim and hold." At first reading, this appears to be a socialist attack on the educational advantages enjoyed by an economic elite who in turn would offer the disadvantaged just enough education "to enlighten the poor about their predestined inferiority." And in other passages, Illich appears to have joined the political left in its assault on the military-industrial-educational complex: "The myth of universal education, the ritual of compulsory schooling, and a professional structure erected to ensure the progress of the technocrat reinforce one another." But Illich in fact is more properly associated with the educational values of the counterculture that Kozol complained about, and with the ecclesiastical rejection of secular progress. On closer examination, his vision idealizes a future society in which the dominant ethic will not be economic justice and equality but rather the virtue of poverty. Thus he wrote, in a revealing article in the *Christian Century,* that "we can not tolerate any further complicity on the part of Christian churches in the worship of the idol of progress." He said that deschooling is merely a first step, and that a church might recognize the breakdown of schools but still be committed to "the myth of general education as a consumer commodity." Such a church "will argue for disestablishment of the schools, for more equal distribution of educational resources, and for protection of the unschooled against discrimination on the job or in society, and in consequence it will certainly be welcomed into the company of 'progressive' movements." But such a church will remain the accomplice of a consumer society and "a Pharaoh who snares new slaves into a world which technocracy renders ever more impersonal, opaque, and polluted." But a church can go beyond mere deschooling. "It can go back to Christianity's purest tradition and announce the coming of the Kingdom which is not of this Earth, the Kingdom whose mystery we are privileged to know. Those who want to follow Jesus must make this choice, even though the church they belong to bows the knee to the Baal of 'progress.' In the name of God we must denounce idolatry of progress, the constant escalation of production which pollutes our planet. We must expose the pseudo-theology of a kind of education that only prepares its pupils for a life of frustrating consumption."

Illich, in other words, is basically committed to the more-is-less doctrine of the counterculture, to the zero-growth policy of the Club of Rome, and to the antisecular theology of the Church of Rome. And while he has had his difficulties with the Vatican, he could hardly be charged with the heresy of modernism. His educational reforms are intended not to make the poor richer but the rich poorer. "It makes no sense to propose a minimum income unless you define a maximum one—nobody can ever get enough who does not know what is enough. It makes no sense to advocate minimum levels of health care, transport, and access to tools unless you define maximum levels of medical treatment, speed, and bigness." He called for "the liberation of the world from the idols of progress, development, efficiency, Gross National Product, and Gross National Education." That world today consists of the Babel of Russia, the Egypt of the United States, and the Desert of the Third World. As for the people who live in that Third World, Illich conceded they could probably use "slightly better tools." But he advised them nevertheless to remain in the desert, with the living God, and to avoid the fleshpots of both Egypt and Babel. "Liberation can come only from those who, having been set free, choose the desert." Illich thus proclaims "the blessedness of the poor" and solicits an "antitechnocratic consensus" which he said "translates very easily into the need for voluntary poverty as it was preached by the Lord."

One can only wonder what a maximum level of medical treatment would be. And the quotations cited may explain why Kozol has said: "I find myself in the difficult position of one who admires Ivan Illich and respects Everett Reimer, but who also lives in Boston in the year of 1972." The kind of de-schooling that Illich advocates also would probably be hard to sell in Harlem or Chile.

But there are, fortunately, methods to reduce and reform schooling without abolishing it altogether, and a number of these have been suggested by the Carnegie Foundation and a task force appointed by the Department of Health, Education, and Welfare. They include counseling programs to discourage reluctant students from entering college, or from remaining in college once they have entered. Indeed changes in the draft law already have had an effect on enrollment pressures. Other recommendations include the creation of a national youth service, college credits for community-service activities, federal subsidies for off-campus study, apprenticeship training, new job opportunities, more emphasis on special degrees such as the two-year associate of arts, and an accelerated program of year-round studies and qualifying examinations that would enable a student to earn his bachelor's degree in three years in-stead of four. In addition, of course, there already has been the phenomenal growth of two-year community colleges.

There are a number of reasons why a reduction of schooling would be advantageous at the level of higher education. Colleges and universities are in a financial crisis, their costs going up while their incomes decline, and some of the reforms just mentioned presumably would alleviate the problem. The other alternatives are further increases in tuitions, which are already out of sight for many families, or increased state and federal financial assistance, which might not be forthcoming. Many young people, as noted, are not happy in school and might feel more at ease if they were productively employed in apprenticeship programs or on-the-job training (as they would have been in medieval society, before the invention of schools and the psychosocial identity crisis). The Sputnik scare resulted in educational overkill, and graduate schools are turning out far more Ph.D.s than the economy can possibly absorb —especially with the cutback in government and industrial research. Similarly, schools of education have been training additional teachers to instruct an elementary-school population that is shrinking in size as a result of a birth rate that has been declining since 1957. (And failure of the education schools to anticipate the present teacher surplus, which hardly required a crystal ball, has inspired some critics to propose the creation of a federal agency that would predict future manpower needs and might even be authorized to regulate the pattern of college enrollments.) Finally, accordingly to a study by the Com-mission on Human Resources, more than 25 percent of the students now in college will be going into jobs that do not really require a college education.

The actual percentage is probably even higher. But while a great number of high-status jobs do not require a college education, they usually do require a college *degree*. And it is this emphasis on educational certification ("the tyranny of diplomaism") that makes hash of most efforts to reduce the amount of schooling in America. It also explains one of Kozol's main objections to Illich. While he agrees with Illich that the credential apparatus represents illegal job discrimination, Kozol adds that "we must face up to the hard truth that these credentials and measured areas of expertise and certified ability constitute, *as of now,* the irreducible framework of our labor and our struggle." So we can not simply turn our backs and act as if the system of credentials will disappear. "The citadel does not need to be revered or loved in order to be stormed and conquered. It is insane, however, to behave as though it were not there."

According to Michael Harrington: "America is becoming a 'knowledge economy' in which higher and higher educational credentials are required (sometimes unnecessarily) in order to get a good job." As a socialist, he attributes the failure of poor children to obtain those jobs to a class structure that denies the poor "effective access to tax-supported education and works to make deprivation both self-perpetuating and hereditary." And if the failure of poor children is traced to the fact that they score low on IQ tests, Harrington will not settle for the standard liberal argument that such tests merely reflect the "middle-class bias" of the tests. Rather, he refers to the studies by Christopher Jencks and David Riesman in *The Academic Revolution.* To those who assert the IQ tests are unfair to the poor, Jencks and Riesman replied: "Life is unfair to the poor. Tests are merely the results. Urban middle-class in general and professional work in particular seem to nourish potential academic skills and interests in parents, while lower-class life does the opposite. . . . So long as the distribution of power and privilege remains radically unequal, so long as some children are raised by adults at the bottom while others are raised by adults at the top, the children will more often than not turn out unequal."

This raises the question of heredity and environment as determining factors in the production of intelligence. And the argument that heredity is the primary factor has been made most recently by scholars such as Arthur Jensen, William Shockley, and Richard J. Herrnstein. These arguments in turn have been examined in a very perceptive study by David K. Cohen, professor of education and director of the Center for Educational Policy Research at Harvard University.

While Herrnstein at least pointed out the danger of generalizing from individual to group differences, said Cohen, his conclusions nevertheless "questioned the traditional liberal idea that stupidity results from the inheritance of poverty, contending instead that poverty results from the inheritance of stupidity." And then Cohen put his finger directly on the problem, observing: "It is hard to figure out whether poverty causes low IQ or low IQ causes poverty, because they tend to occur in the same persons. The very people who are continually suspected of being genetically underendowed with respect to IQ have also been socially underendowed with respect to environment." While he did not dismiss the possibility or importance of genetic differences, however, Cohen proceeded to a more tractable question: "whether, and how much, IQ counts in America in terms of status and power."

This question has deeply concerned humanist scholars and general intellectuals who have been fired up by the assertion of political scientist Zbigniew Brzezinski that power in a technetronic society will be held by a scientific elite—a "meritocratic few" who have the brains necessary to understand the new electronic-computer language. And although he did not deal directly with Brzezinski himself, Cohen did come up with data casting doubt on that basic assumption.

Cohen found, for example, that tested ability and inherited socio-economic status are roughly equal in gaining entrance to college; that ability and status combined explain less than half the actual variation in college attendance; that other factors include motivation, luck, discrimination, chance, and family encouragement or lack of it—and that as far as the latter factor is concerned, "lots of poor parents push their children very hard, and lots of non-poor parents don't." Among poor students in roughly the same family circumstances, more brains means a much better chance of going to college; among rich students, more brains also increases the chances of going to college, but in their case measured intelligence is only slightly more important than family status. "This is a great deal different from a world in which going to college is wholly determined by family position, but it is far from a world in which going to college is wholly determined by intellectual ability."

In any case, all other things being equal, IQ seems to have little or no effect on the kinds of jobs people obtain as adults; among people with the same educations and socio-economic backgrounds, a higher IQ does not help them get a higher status job. Once a student leaves college, his grades have no relation to his income or occupational status; the most productive workers who are highly rated by their supervisors do not in general have higher IQs than other workers. In short, "nowhere can we find any empirical support for the idea that brains are becoming increasingly more important to status in America.'"

What really counts in occupational attainment is not raw IQ but the length of time one spends in school. As opposed to a meritocracy based on intellect, therefore, we may be creating a "school-ocracy." Additional educational requirements for certification or licensing in turn appear to be a way of "professionalizing" an occupation and thereby enhancing its respectability. And this can have unhappy consequences including "the subversion of the legitimate purposes of educational institutions" and the creation of a job selection system "in which the ability to remain glued to the seat of a chair for long periods of time becomes a prime recommendation for advancement."

Cohen also suggested that such a system might make it impossible to tap the unique talents of various ethnic groups, as Edward T. Hall recommended in Chapter Seven. In the past, the occupational avenues selected by different ethnic groups may have reflected "cultural and historical differences from group to group with regard to the sorts of work which were known and esteemed in the parent country." But to the extent that schooling now determines occupational entry or advancement, "it may close off genuine cultural differences in occupational values, and irrationally stifle alternatives which might otherwise flourish. To the extent that success in a homogeneous system of schooling becomes the *sine qua non* of entry to occupations, cultural diversity in conceptions of success and worthy work may be diminished."

Since intellectuals are always complaining that they have little power or influence, said Cohen, it comes as a surprise to hear that intellectuals are now in danger of having too much power. "But if holding political office, for instance, is an index of power, it is hard to see any cause for alarm, for there certainly is no evidence of an undue concentration of raw IQ among the ranks of government officials." And his analysis lends weight to Michael W. Miles's assertion, in *The Radical Probe*, that power has not been passed to Brzezinski's meritocratic technicians; power is still wielded by generalists and not by specialists. "Managers, not technicians, dispose of technical resources," wrote Miles, "while politicians, not their advisors, make political decisions."

Cohen added that people with more schooling tend to have somewhat higher incomes, but not in all cases: "lots of jobs with rather high status—preaching, teaching, and the like—don't come with cushy salaries, and lots of jobs with rather low status, like being a plumber or a machinist, do." And he concluded America is not a meritocracy, in the sense it is a society in which income, status, and power are largely determined by IQ. On the contrary, "something we often incorrectly identify with IQ—schooling—seems to be a much more important determinant of adult success than IQ. If getting through school is a mark of merit, then America is moderately meritocratic." But in any case: "Being stupid is not what is responsible for being poor in America."

Discussing the theories of Shockley and others, Skinner said:

"I'm interested in what can be done with the human species as it exists. And whether more is determined by genetic endowment or environmental history I'm in no position to say, and I don't think the facts make this clear. But what I'm very much concerned with is that most of what we *do* is determined by the environment. These people like to use identical twins as an example—reared apart, with identical IQs. But if you take identical twins and raise one, let us say, in China and one in England, the one in China will speak Chinese, the one in England will speak English. And they'll *think* differently. Because the Chinese language encourages one kind of thinking; English language encourages another kind of thinking. And what they do during the day is almost completely determined by their environment, you see, regardless of what there may be in the way of genetic difference. I don't rule out the possibility of genetic differences; they certainly exist among individuals, quite apart from races. You have very bright people and very dull people. There's no basis for mistreating them—the slow, dull people. The white population doesn't mistreat those members of its group who have low IQ as now measured. As I've done myself with the retarded, you try to work out an environment in which they're trained to be reasonably successful. I'm an environmentalist, and I'm on the side of what can be done with the environment. And I would say none of us is developing more than 10 per cent of his potential anyway. And we'd have a better world if we weren't wrestling with these questions all the time—we'd do a lot more than we're doing now."

But what will happen if we work out an environment—a postscarcity economy—in which everybody will be successful, and there is nothing to do, or at least nothing that has to be done. What will happen after the abolition not of compulsory education but of compulsory labor? What will we do then, when the banner reads simply "to each according to his needs"?

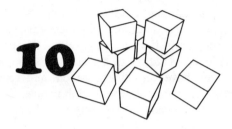

10

We enter in the midst of a heated exchange between a young girl, Robin, and an older businessman named Gordon. They are concerned about the value of work in modern America.

Robin:	*I don't feel that strong and weak are the dimensions that you should judge people. Strong and weak is cruel and aggressive. I want other things to be valued. I want the weak person who is kind and gentle and doesn't harm people to be the one everybody respects and values.*
Gordon:	*But this breeds mediocrity. You will not have a dynamic country as you now have. It shows that the person had a drive. It showed that he had something that he worked for.*
Robin:	*I think that these drives should be put into better things than getting money for your own self. You're avoiding the conditions that exist in the country and how work isn't available for some people and how there hasn't been the kind of training that might be available or the kinds of options that other people have and therefore, there's a pounding down of certain people in this society.*
Gordon:	*O.K., there's a pounding down and there's also a granting to some minority groups and they don't fulfill the grant. They don't try their hardest. They want it now. They don't want to work for it. If somebody cannot work for something you can't give it out to them freely. It's got to be earned.*
Robin:	*It's a funny thing that you bring up this work ethic which is part of our country. Does work mean a man's worth? Whatever he can produce? Is that really it?*
Gordon:	*You have to give some work somehow. How can you pay people? People today can earn more money for not working and they will do that. They have no sense of responsibility*

	whatsoever. They should be contributing to society as long as they have the money.
Robin:	*I think if you could fulfill them to contribute to society they would. And I think that's the whole point of this: it doesn't.*
Gordon:	*You're going to work for what you get. Today people are paid by you or me. We are supporting those that are having a good time . . .*
Robin:	*Do you think people should work for 10¢ an hour?*
Gordon:	*Yes.*
Robin:	*And live on it?*
Gordon:	*No. What they don't make, they should be given but they have to do something to get it.*
Robin:	*I think the problem is not who's working and how much you're paying but the fact that before people even grow up they have already been influenced so that they don't care about contributing to society because they know guys like you are not gonna let them get any further anyway. There's a whole class like Howard Hughes who are living off of surplus labor. They're living off of other people's work.*
Gordon:	*Can you tell me whether you're really against this or are you jealous?*
Robin:	*I think that any system where one man exploits another man by living off of his wages and living on somebody elses wages is an evil to society.*
Gordon:	*It's based on wages. What do you expect to do, go down to the store and say 'I need a loaf of bread' and just pick it up and take it off?*
Robin:	*You seem to think that work is how you identify your life and is the major consideration. You should spend a lot of time on it and be dedicated to it. Part of my philosophy—and I think a lot of other people are going to take this position—is that work isn't the only thing we want to do in life. We want to do other things we want to work on and that's building families together or cooperative living or similar goals.*

10.
The Kingdom of Freedom

A curious thing has happened to the characters in the plays written by students at the Yale Drama School. They are all unemployed.

This has puzzled the school's administrative dean, Howard Stein, who said: "When I began to teach playwriting, the first question I could ask a student was what his character did for a living. 'What's his work?' And the student would tell me. 'He sells birds.' But you could never ask that question now. Never! Because the work now means nothing—absolutely nothing."

Or everything—absolutely everything.

The future of the work ethic was probably the most important issue raised by the youth counterculture, and it has survived the collapse of the counterculture itself. In spite of the economic recession, it seems to preoccupy the thinking of young people on college campuses and industrial assembly lines.

"People are so afraid of getting themselves into patterns," said the Oberlin coed we quoted earlier. "They're so afraid of establishing the Willie Loman kind of life where you don't have anything outside it: where you're always on trains or you have to commute every day. The idea of 9-to-5 is the big bugaboo in colleges today."

"It's interesting when you ask a student for some idea about the constant reality in his play," said Stein. "It doesn't have to be a representational reality. It's like the foul lines in a ball field, and I don't care where the hell they are—just so they're somewhere. But it's very tough to get students to articulate this, because the students are between heaven and earth."

The students actually are located somewhere between a scarcity and a post-scarcity economy. During the affluence of the 1960s, they lived for a brief time in a postscarcity subculture, subsidized by their parents, and they have retained the vision of a leisure society where work will be transformed, if not indeed eliminated. They are more realistic now. They realize this vision lies far in the future, at least for most people, and the recession if anything relieved the emotional pressure of dealing with leisure or choosing from a wide variety of available work options. But they also realize the fundamental problem has merely been postponed, and it continues to fascinate them.

This fascination is reflected in some of the books they are reading. Many are reading Hegel. Many more are reading science fiction. And one explanation of the science fiction boom is suggested by Hayden White, who said:

"Science fiction imagines a utopian world of the future, and it appeals to conditions of work that are no longer possible in our modern technological society. In the typical science fiction novel, for example, there is no real distinction between the place where the scientist works and the place where he lives. Secondly, it's not work that's divided up between daytime work and nighttime work. It's not work that's disassociated from the life that one leads. It's not alienated labor that the scientist performs. He's as dedicated as a priest. Thirdly, the relationship of the young scientist to the senior scientist—which is always crucial—is that of the father and son engaged in common work in these kind of home conditions. And usually the scientist father figure has a beautiful daughter who becomes part of the scientist's family. Not only that, the scientist always loves his work. His recreation is his work, and the reverse. It's a kind of craft image—even a village conception of both family relationships and the relationship between work and family and recreation. It's a return to a mythic world of work and life that these students think existed in the village and in the integrated family. And my students are disenchanted with school because it's work-oriented in terms of the present socio-economic structure. The university takes those existing options of work and labor for granted and then tries to supply technicians for them. And the students repudiate that—at least intellectually. And that's often what they mean now by their socialism. My students will no longer accept the present work options as that by which they will define their own sense of self, in the way that their fathers did. And what many of them tell me is that they must find a moral equivalent to work."

If students are attracted to science fiction by an archaic notion of a master-apprentice type of work, Hegel attracts them in part because he deals with the master-slave relationship. White said: "Hegel was really the first person to deal with the concept of a proletariat, which he called the rabble of poverty. And many students identify with this rabble of poverty because they have the advantage—in the students' eyes—of being excluded from the present work

options. That's one reason so many students emulate the poor and the disadvantaged—the way they dress, their life styles. That's why students idealize
the black family and ghetto family life. That kind of life is supposed to be
warm and intimate, because these people aren't taken away from their homes
and their loved ones by work. They don't have jobs."

Three Harvard and Radcliffe students—Sue, Rick, and E. J.—talked about
work in a discussion that lasted far into the night in Adams House in Cambridge. Significantly, the session began with a debate over women's liberation
and the division of labor in the contemporary family.

"Liberation," said E. J., "seems to suggest two careerist people who are
out for themselves, who really want to make it in the bourgeois world. And
that would be a disaster. Society is too aggressive and competitive as it is,
what with all the men out pushing their careers. Bourgeois liberation is just
women becoming men. And then we'll have a society in which everybody is
aggressive. And I'd like to know what'll happen to children and family life
in that kind of world."

"Take the woman I would want to hitch up with," said Rick. "I'm not interested in both of us having good careers. I'd like an arrangement where she
could work some if she wanted to, and I for my part could get more involved
in a home life. And neither of us would have a career that's a heavy-duty
thing, the way it is now. So much of liberation is women who are trying to
be careerists. And I'd like to be spared from careerism."

"That's just the point," said Sue. "You have to redefine what a career can
be. It could be five hours a day instead of eight. Or four hours a day."

"To change the division of labor in the family," said Rick, "you'd have to
change the division of labor in the work force. You'd have to reconstruct it so
people could work half days or something like that. And that's one reason
you don't have so many crazies running around now saying we should get rid
of the machines. Because we need technology and affluence to liberate us from
drudgery."

"It doesn't depend on affluence," said Sue. "You have to work out some
way where two people together could do everything there is to be done—earning a living, taking care of a home. And the two people would share all those
chores between them. Maybe they'd each spend four hours a day earning a
living and four hours a day doing the housework."

"Fine," said Rick. "But that means you can't have suburban living and city
jobs where it takes two hours a day commuting. It would be ridiculous to
have two people working half days in that situation, because they'd be absent
from the children too much. You'd have to get jobs closer to home and build
more of a community."

"Agreed," said E. J. "That's why I said two careerists working a 40-hour
week or more would be absolute disaster. And a 20-hour week would be a big

improvement, because everybody would have more time then to devote to community and family and self-improvement."

"But I still say we need more technology to accomplish that," said Rick. "And the work itself should still be meaningful. I mean, let the machines take out the drudgery so the work we do can be more creative. I was reading a book that told how churches were built in the Middle Ages, for example, and it said a big crew of workmen would cut out the stones in rough-hewn shapes. Then artists and craftsmen would finish them off in pleasing shapes. So why don't we use our machines to make rough-hewn rocks, and let people do the creative part?"

That was an interesting conversation, and it tends to support the theory proposed in earlier chapters: that some of the apparent assaults directed against the family are actually inspired by a desire to restore or revitalize that institution, not to destroy it, and that women's liberation in particular could ultimately help to serve that purpose—transforming not only the present family structure but also our dominant attitudes toward work and the public sector of society. One of the few scholars I know who seems to have made this connection is the historian Christopher Lasch, who has written that revival of the "woman question" is intimately connected to the central issue of contemporary domestic politics—control of the corporation—and that the possible emergence of a new kind of labor movement in turn "would require a change not only in attitudes toward work but in attitudes toward leisure, consumption, and domestic life." Lasch observed that the family more than any other institution has expressed the separation between work and the rest of life, and he added: "The precarious political and economic stability that was re-established after the Great Depression rested as heavily on a rehabilitation of domesticity . . . as it did on military spending. The arrangement whereby private consumption compensates for loss of autonomy at work, and for the absence of a vigorous public and communal life, depended on a new sentimentalization of the family, in which the nineteenth-century cult of domesticity was refurbished with images of the suburb as a refuge from the city."

In short, most labor today—especially for industrial workers—has become almost totally meaningless. It has lost its intrinsic value as a self-rewarding mode of activity and is now, at best, simply a means to an end. It is a way to make money in order to purchase consumer goods, or commodities, and the modern family for its part has become little more than the basic economic unit designed to consume all those commodities. In theory, family life was supposed to compensate the worker for the meaningless toil resulting from the division of labor; thus the concept of man's home as his castle—or, in Max Horkheimer's term, a "realm of freedom," outside the workshop, where he could lead a rich inner life in the company of his loved ones. In fact, however, after hours of unfulfilling labor, man returns to the castle with his brain benumbed, and his rich inner life consists of watching television (which informs him, for the most part, about the new commodities available). He yells at his wife (who yells back), scolds the children, and possibly benumbs his brain still more (with beer or martinis, depending on his self-image of social status). Worse yet, he does not recognize the relationship between what happens to him at work and what happens to him when he comes home. Even if he lives in a happy castle, when he looks down from the ramparts he sees the castle surrounded by slums and angry poor people and desperate people who might well rob or kill him on his way to work. Also, the air stinks. But he fails to recognize the relationship between what he does at work and all of these factors—in other words, the starvation of the public sector that Galbraith talked about.

It is in this sense that Lasch has described *"the fatal split between home and work"* as the basic cause of a system "under which people are in effect compensated for loss of dignity and autonomy at work by increased leisure and higher wages to spend on consumer goods and leisure-time activities." He added: "It is because work is seen merely as a means to something else, instead of an intrinsically satisfying and necessary activity, that people no longer concern themselves with its social consequences. The auto worker who drives long distances to work along choked highways, under polluted skies, suffers directly from the social consequences of the automobile. But his union does not concern itself with those consequences or with the corporate policies that help to bring them about; nor does the worker dream that he himself might have something to say about what use is made of the cars he produces, or about better ways to produce less harmful cars. To him the production of cars is his means of support, nothing more."

As Edward T. Hall said, young people today know something is wrong but not necessarily what is wrong, and they therefore in many cases aim their attacks at the wrong targets. Thus current criticisms of the nuclear family very often confuse cause and effect, blaming the family for the alienation and unhappiness that actually are the result of working conditions for which family life is supposed to compensate. Modern family life, however, can not compensate for those conditions, and the only solution is to change the nature of work, and to change it in such a way that family life in consequence also is transformed. That is what many of the more thoughtful young people are talking about, and women's liberation in this context translates into family liberation, social liberation, human liberation. It means the liberation of women from the sterile isolation of contemporary housewifery, allowing them to engage in creative and meaningful work; and it also means the liberation of men from equally sterile careers, allowing them to become husbands, fathers, good neighbors, involved citizens, and creative individuals—both at home and at work.

Instead of making an effort to change the conditions of work, many young people in the late 1960s attempted to liberate themselves from careerism simply by dropping out. Affluent students at the so-called elite universities dropped out of school, dropped out of society, and joined the counterculture.

"I don't know exactly what they had in mind," said Martin Peretz. "I suppose some of them thought they could live off the counterculture, or that income wouldn't matter in the new society they were going to build. These were the people who normally would have gone into the houses of finance and the Wall Street law firms. Many of them thought that because they seemed at least to be dropping off the career ladders, the command posts of American society would wither without them. Alas, they found there were plenty of students from less elegant schools and less affluent backgrounds who had lots of ambition to climb up those ladders and take over the command posts. And that's exactly what happened—not really the 'blueing of America' that some people predicted, but to some extent at least a 'circulation of elites' in which the entire society really opened up in a way: a democratic process which I think in the long-run perspective of society was a very desirable development. As for the dropouts, some of them seemed just to have vanished, and I think there's a discernibly lost generation. But since the command posts didn't cripple, a lot of them have come back to school. And these people are now worrying about their careers in rather traditional ways—that is, personal gratification, even income expectations. Of course, a large part of that obviously was the recession—and also the closing off of the university as an obviously attractive place in which to work: obviously attractive in terms of economics and teaching. But I've had a number of seniors talk to me about income expectations. And these are questions that one had not really heard from students for three or four years."

But Lasch believes at least some of the dropouts have returned to school with the intention of changing their professions from within, and that belief is shared by Michael Harrington. "I think these kids are different," Harrington said, referring not only to the drops-ins but to the total college population. "But they're not going to be different merely as students on a campus. If that's all that's involved, it's not an enormous thing. It's important, but not tremendously important. But I think their existence is a reflection of a change in class structure and attitudes where they're going to go out in the society and be teachers—be different kinds of lawyers, different kinds of doctors, different kinds of engineers. So I think these kids are going to be different kinds of adults. And I think that's the key hope." Lasch in fact has asked: "Is it possible that these stirrings in the professions foreshadow a more general movement of people at their work, trying to turn their work into something at once more satisfying and less deleterious in its social effects—a new kind of labor movement?"

Lasch sees the genesis of such a movement in the "industrialization of higher education," referred to in the last chapter, that created deteriorating conditions of work in the university and in the "knowledge industry" in general. An increasing number of intellectual workers face declining autonomy, regimentation, and loss of status. "Many," said Lasch, "will sink to the level of the intellectual proletariat, swelling the already growing numbers of teachers, low level civil servants, public employees, and clerical workers, among whom there have already been signs of labor unrest, as in the stirrings among young schoolteachers against city bureaucracies and their own unions. Their common subordination to bureaucratic control may overcome the many barriers between the professional and technical strata and the new working class, bringing into being a new labor movement." And the new labor movement would not be like traditional trade unionism. Rather, it would seek control of the intellectual product; it would deeply concern itself with the social consequences of that production; it would assert "a determination to see work in its relation to all phases of community life," and its aim would be "to change the structures of powerful institutions by challenging prevailing modes of work." Lasch concluded: "The mere existence of a student movement and of young graduates who are carrying its attitudes into corporations, professions, and bureaucracies . . . is one reason to think that the private corporation may yet find itself confronted with a powerful challenge to its very existence."

That last passage has a familiar ring, recalling Galbraith's naive faith in the "conscience" of the modern corporation in which control has passed from the owners to a socially enlightened management. The private corporation remains a bureaucracy that has as its primary function the production, above all else, of a profit. It is virtually impossible to prevent a bureaucracy from at least trying to do what it was designed to do—that is inherent in the very nature of all bureaucracies—and I can not share Lasch's hope that his new labor movement is the solution to the capitalist dilemma of allowing profit-oriented corporations to make major social decisions. But I do share Harrington's distrust of the left's continued effort to find a substitute proletariat—in Lasch's case, the new class of professional and technical workers (who also are reminiscent of the "petty-bourgeois socialists" derided in *The Communist Manifesto*).

Besides, there is no need to search for a substitute proletariat. Erosion of the work ethic and open rebellion find their most dramatic expression today among the traditional proletarians—the working class, and especially the young production workers who have adopted the long hair of the counterculture and much of its philosophy. Absenteeism is a serious problem, as is the job turnover rate, and the young workers in some cases have been accused of engaging in industrial sabotage to express their frustrations. Marx said that worker alienation was inevitable with the division of labor and the production of commodities—a commodity being a product that is made for consumption by somebody else, not the person who made it. And such alienation is accentuated by the monotony of the repetitious and fragmented labor that is characteristic of the assembly line production introduced in 1914 by Henry Ford. Blue collar youth has revolted against this system—the most emphatic example being the 1972 strike at the Vega assembly plant run by the General Motors Corporation at Lordstown, Ohio, where it was charged that a speedup had allowed each worker about thirty-six seconds to perform his assigned operation.

Irving Levine's ethnic project has concentrated on the problems of production workers aged 18 to 24. Discussing those problems, he said:

"In a sense, the counterculture is dead because it's now a part of the conventional culture. I mean, it raised real questions as to whether work is the end-all and be-all, and those questions are so deep that they've penetrated the whole society. They certainly got through to the young people, and now we've got a mass base of young workers who no longer believe in production for production's sake, and you can't bullshit them on the assembly line about this being a good way of life. Because it goes all the way up to management, as a matter of fact, and it's all sensed. There's a breakdown in the seriousness with which the so-called values of a corporation are pursued, so that license in a way has come into the situation. For example, planned obsolescence. The moment that idea was introduced into the work ethic, by management, what did that mean to the value system of the worker? He knew he was turning out a lousy product. He was embarrassesd by it. He couldn't be proud of his work. He wasn't even going to buy the product himself, because he knew it stunk. So that helped to break down the norm of the workplace, which was rather rigid and conforming and dedicated to Puritanism. It's also broken down among the executives. Golf at two, you know. Time off. Weekends in the country. Airplanes. These were direct signals from top management, that life had changed, and it's penetrated to the ranks. And another thing has been the introduction of black cultural forms into the workplace: a certain amount of looseness, and less rigid habits, and less obeisance to authority. So you had young Catholic girls, for example, who had been telephone operators and stuck to their knitting and were good soldiers. And then you had the introduction of blacks who were less restrained in the way they spoke and acted and so forth. And there was an initial resentment, of course, but then these little Catholic girls began asking questions: 'Why am I so crazy? What am I involved in this kind of a bag for? These people seem to be having much more fun. They're much more alive. And they're getting away with it, too. So why shouldn't I?'

"So the quality of the product is devalued. And the process of creating the product is dehumanized. And everybody is replaceable. So if you don't come, somebody else does your work. You can take Monday off, you can take Friday off, and you don't suffer too many consequences. But you do sense a great sense of loss of your relative importance. So maybe you don't come in at all. I think Chrysler, for example, at one point was losing 4,000 employees a year who put in one day and quit—out of a work force of about 65,000—and I don't know what the statistics were for the second day, third day, or a week; it must have been phenomenal. And the kids can afford to do this because many of them are maybe living off the relative affluence of the family. They can afford to do it up to the age of 25, at least. And that's the magic year. That's when their merit increases stop, and they begin to lose real income because of marriage and kids and the limits of their education, and they don't have enough seniority yet to stave off layoffs. It's the age when a certain amount of fatalism begins to set in about settling down. You know: 'This is going to be my life.' It's the age where you're probably going to get the most feeling of alienation, I think. At the younger age there's hope, idealism, even when it's masked by a sort of phony-aggressive, I-don't-care attitude. Twenty-five is the age where there are signs you're not going to do too much better than you're doing. And I think that's a very dangerous, difficult age."

Major American employers have made some efforts to cure the assembly line blues for young workers and old, creating a variety of "job enrichment" programs. For example, an automobile company spokesman said: "At one plant we allow the guys to paint the machines they work on any color they want." A greater effort has been devoted to building up overseas operations, in anticipation perhaps of the day when nobody will show up for work.

One of the more interesting attempts to reduce alienation has been introduced on an experimental basis in Sweden at a new plant designed to assemble engines for the Saab-99 sedan. Industrial robots do much of the monotonous labor, and finished parts are sent to assembly teams of four workers. A single team member can assemble an entire engine by himself, if he chooses, while other members may decide to work in pairs or in three-man combinations.

But automation continues to reduce the proportion of workers who are actually involved in production, and America has already developed a post-industrial economy (defined as an economy in which most workers are employed in service industries as opposed to production). In addition, the long-range trend has been toward increased leisure as a result of early retirement, longer vacations, and a shorter work week. According to many forecasters— who in fact express the final goal of socialism—the ultimate trend is toward abolition of compulsory labor. In short, "retirement at birth."

The ultimate question, then, is how such a future society would cope with boundless leisure. There might be an instructive example in the experience of the counterculture, epitomized by the Woodstock rock festival in 1969. And an informed observer of that experience is Michael Wadleigh, who (as mentioned) won an Oscar for his film report on Woodstock.

"I'm afflicted myself with the Protestant ethic," he said. "I have an orientation that makes me want to work at something, and I have no trouble finding things; my art is my work. But I found myself surrounded by young people who had a great deal of difficulty in defining what they wanted to do—and once having defined it, had real difficulty getting themselves in line to do it. The drug scene, the dropout scene. They'd buy a farm, but couldn't get the crops in. And the tragic thing is, they desperately wanted both the motivation and control over themselves to do something. The main thing was, they were just incredibly unhappy. They were extraordinarily unhappy. Their sense of apathy was a terrible, terrible thing. And I think it was due to their tremendous potential of choices. God, the number of people attracted to us there was legion. And God, I heard it from kid after kid. 'Please help me define myself. Please put me in some channel. Let me thread your projector. Anything. Because I'm faced with so many choices, I'm deactivated.'

"And it isn't just kids who can't handle leisure. I also made a film at the auto stamping plants in Detroit. And there was this one guy there, he made me want to cry. He had this menial job, the same thing day after day. And he told me: 'I make a good living. I got a home, a color TV, a boat. I got everything prescribed for me. But you know what I want? I want a hobby. I think my mind is destroyed.' And every five years he got a six-week vacation. He'd take his boat to some lake, and he'd water ski. Which is a vacuous recreation, because it has so few variables, and the heroes of the lake are the people who can ski on their bare feet. And that's it. So he'd go round in circles. And this was his big attempt to channel himself into something rewarding. And every year he'd voluntarily come back to work after two weeks. And the company finally had to start a training program on how to use the six weeks. They literally had vacation classes. And I think society in the future will have to help these people deal with themselves. Especially the schools. They'll have to teach people how to live, now how to earn a living."

Hayden White recalled discussions with student activists at UCLA. "They told me," he said, "that what is killing this country is work that does not produce the person but produces something outside the person. And the real problem is to make creative people. Or the real problem is to create yourself, produce yourself. This means they want to destroy the distinction between work and play. And they want all men to be artists, in the sense that the artist is a man whose work is himself. But they don't mean the kind of art you and I talk about. And that's why the pop art thing was very important. What pop art said was, we must end the distinction between high art and craft."

It remains to be asked if all men can be artists. Marx thought they could, and indeed he predicted as much in the era after the abolition of labor which he called the Kingdom of Freedom, "where the development of man's powers becomes an end in itself, a realm which can only bloom on the basis of the realm of necessity. The shortening of the working day is its fundamental premise." But Marx did not elaborate; he lacks an adequate psychology of leisure— and that is what many students are trying to locate now in his predecessor Hegel.

A deeper question is whether it is in man's nature to work at all, in any capacity, unless forced to.

The pioneer sociologist Max Weber proposed that man "by nature" used to quit working as soon as he had earned enough to satisfy his essential needs. Weber suggested that man's mind had been warped by Puritan morality (the Protestant ethic), which made work a virtue in itself and thus laid the basis for the development of modern capitalism. But this is generally regarded now as a simplistic formula, and Weber himself acknowledged "it would also further be necessary to investigate how Protestant Asceticism was in turn influenced in its development and its character by the totality of social conditions, especially economic." He also made clear that the Protestant ethic did not idealize meaningless toil. "What God demands is not labour in itself, but rational labour in a calling."

In that last conversation before his death, Saul Alinsky repeated his assertion he would like to go to hell—so he could organize all those people down there. And he discussed the concept of leisure in terms of his anti-ideological politics.

"I've never bought ideology," he said. "Because ideology gives you the security of a definite answer. Let's take the Marxist ideology, that all our troubles are due to the exploitation of the proletariat by the capitalists. So we have a revolution, and now we're in a political paradise. But guys like myself don't believe there is a political paradise on earth. And I never meant anything so completely as I did when I said that the pursuit of happiness is endless. Happiness lies in the pursuit. We're never going to catch up on the thing, you know, and that's beautiful, too; that's life. Can you imagine a world in which you had all these things settled? That's one reason one of the guys that I dedicated *Rules* to was the first known radical I could find, the first guy to take on the establishment and score, a guy by the name of Lucifer. You know, I can see him sitting there, in the words of the Greek philosopher, saying: 'Jesus Christ, you've seen one beatific vision, you've seen them all. What the fuck am I supposed to do, sit here ad infinitum looking at these goddamn visions? I wonder what the hell's out there?' You know.

"You recall that old Mark Twain remark about people who spend all their time trying to get into heaven for eternity when they don't know what in hell to do on a rainy Sunday afternoon? They'd go crazy, up there forever."

Alinsky also suggested that what drives man is not so much the need to work or the need for a calling as the need to seek some form of stress or tension, as a man might seek stress by climbing a mountain—not to conquer the mountain, as the popular conception would have it, but to conquer himself, to stretch his own limits, to grow, and to become in some ineffable way *more* than he was. "You've got to have tensions," said Alinsky. "Tensions are life. You take all the tensions out—you have a world of peace, love, cooperation, no problems at all—and you know what's going to happen? You're going to have people lined up in front of every psychiatrist's office, and they're going to be asking for treatments to get tensions induced in them. You get to be a goddamn vegetable if you haven't got any tensions. Life itself—everything creative comes out of it, whether it's a Hegelian synthesis or anything else—it's always a tension, whatever it is. So that's why I'd say the pursuit of happiness is better than happiness. The pursuit of anything."

The economist John Maynard Keynes predicted a leisure society—and a widespread nervous breakdown. "I think with dread," he said, "of the readjustment of the habits and instincts of the ordinary man, bred into him for countless generations, which he may be asked to discard within a few decades." The artists—people who can sing—might survive. But, said Keynes, "how few of us can sing."

Freud praised work and said it represents the best way to keep men in contact with reality, but he thought most people have no appetite for it: "No other technique for the conduct of life attaches the individual so firmly to reality as laying emphasis on work; for his work at least gives him a secure place in a portion of reality, in the human community. . . . And yet, as a path to happiness, work is not highly praised by men. They do not strive after it as they do after other possibilities of satisfaction. The great majority of people only work under the stress of necessity, and this natural aversion to work raises most difficult social problems."

Norman O. Brown extended Freud's later theories to hold that man works in order to repress the death instinct, that he keeps busy to blot out the knowledge he is an animal who dies (death, at the saying goes, being nature's way of telling us to slow down). Once he learns to accept death, said Brown, man will be liberated from the neurosis of work. Brown added, ". . . from the Freudian point of view, every ordinary man has tasted the paradise of play in his own childhood. Underneath the habits of work in every man lies the immortal instinct for play. The foundation on which the man of the future will be built is already there, in the repressed unconscious; the foundation does not have to be created out of nothing, but recovered. Nature—or history—is not setting us a goal without endowing us with the equipment to reach it."

There is an obvious danger that a majority of people in a leisure society might turn to hedonism as an antidote to boredom, as occurred in the counterculture, leaving the affairs of state to be managed by those sinister meritocratic technicians who know how to run the computers. But perhaps the fundamental tension involved in the question of leisure is the religious or metaphysical conflict, discussed in Chapter Eight, between the Eastern concept of *being* and the Western concept of *becoming*. Does the Kingdom of God already exist, allowing man to rest in his labors, or has it yet to be achieved? Is it to be OM or Omega? This same conflict was expressed by the atheist Sartre in his distinction, in *Being and Nothingness,* between being-in-itself and being-for-itself.

As William Dunphy summarized that distinction: "Being-in-itself is the being of things (nature, the realm of objects), a self-contained, nontranscending identity that has no meaning because it can not be for-itself. Being-for-itself is the being of consciousness, a perpetual self-transcendence, simultaneously outstripping and falling short of what it can be. The fundamental anxiety of the human condition lies in the uneasiness, the uncertainty of being-for-itself. To repudiate what is radically human and to seek the comfort and security of the status of object, of being-in-itself, is the vision of Hell that Sartre gives us in his play, *No Exit.* There, the three characters are doomed to have their Being as it is in the eyes of others, a state proper to things. The human condition calls rather for heroism. Man's existence, absurd in itself, situated in a meaningless world, acquires meaning only to the extent that man launches free projects to action from the root of his own nothingness."

"It may well be," said Harrington, "in contrast to what Marx thought, that once man stops dying from famines and poverty and starts to die only from death, there will be a resurgence of the religious spirit, not an end to it." And quoting Sidney Hook: "Under Communism, man ceases to suffer as an animal and suffers as a human. He therefore moves from the plane of the pitiful to the plane of the tragic."

In his classic *Work and Its Discontents,* reversing Weber's thesis, Daniel Bell equated man's need to work with a decline in religious belief that gave meaning to life and the hope of immortality. Religion had allowed man to face the problem of death; but with the decline in religious belief there also occurred a decline in the belief in eternal life, and death came to mean the total annihilation of the self. This in turn may have caused "the breakthrough of the irrational which is such a marked feature of the changed moral temper of our times." It may also have caused the modern effort to change the world solely or chiefly through politics rather than transformation of the self. But the fear of death and the terror of the abyss could be staved off by work. Thus work itself became a religion. And it may be that the abolition of work will inspire a new search for religious faith and the evidence of things not seen.

Selected Reading List

CHAPTER ONE

Bell, Daniel

The End of Ideology: On the Exhaustion of Political Ideas in the Fifties.
> With this book, Bell started a debate that still goes on. The book argues that there are no longer any ideological disputes in this country. Free Press, 1960.

Braden, William

The Age of Aquarius.
> The author's earlier discussion of technology and the counterculture. Quadrangle Books, 1970.

Lasch, Christopher

The Agony of the American Left.
> A gifted historian's lament over the failure of The American Left to establish any workable basis for socialism. Random House, Inc., 1969.

O'Neill, William L.

Coming Apart: An Informal History of America in the 1960's.
> Exactly what it claims to be and quite good. Quadrangle Books, 1971.

Roszach, Theodore

The Making of a Counter-Culture.
> A noted scholar peeks at the youth counterculture—"The invasion of centaurs" with a generally sympathetic eye. Doubleday & Co., Inc., 1969.

CHAPTER TWO

Alinsky, Saul

Reveille for Radicals.
> A handbook for radicals by The Old Master which deeply influenced the thought of young radicals and was the first S.D.S. guidebook for action. Random House, Inc., 1969.

Rules for Radicals.
> In which Alinsky upbraids his young followers for misapplying his earlier ideas and then offers some hard-nosed advice on what can be done. Random House, Inc., 1971.

Hofstadter, Richard and Wallace, Michael, (eds.).

American Violence: A Documentary History.
> An excellent study and basic reference source on the subject. Random House, Inc., 1971.

Students for A Democratic Society.

The Port Huron Statement.
> A statement of American ideals as viewed in the early stages of the student movement before everything went sour. 1962.

Commission on Campus Unrest

The Report of The President's Commission on Campus Unrest.
> Rather alarmist report written in a period of chaos but, nevertheless, full of useful facts. It fully details both the Kent State and Jackson State killings. Avon Books.

CHAPTER THREE

Ariès, Philippe

Centuries of Childhood: A Social History of Family Life.
> A classic work that discusses the cultural development of new stages in life and presents a coherent theory on the development of the family. Random House, Inc.

Erikson, Erik H.

Identity, Youth and Crisis.
> One of America's most famous and respected analysts brings together his basic theories regarding the stages of youthful growth. W. W. Norton & Co., Inc. 1968.

Keniston, Kenneth

Young Radicals: Notes on Committed Youth.
> A study of activists in the aspiring social order in which Keniston spells out his theory that we created a new time of life called youth. Harcourt Brace Jovanovich, Inc., 1968.
The Uncommitted: Alienated Youth in American Society.
> Keniston's earlier survey of the drop-out, hippie members of the non-activist, non-committed drug culture. Dell Publishing Co., 1967.

Offer, Daniel

The Psychological World of The Teen-Ager: A Study of Normal Adolescent Boys.
> An eight-year study of two groups of boys which asserts that the generation gap does not exist and that Erikson's "identity crisis" is the exception to the prevailing rule. Basic Books, Inc., 1969.

CHAPTER FOUR

Freud, Sigmund

The Ego and The Id.
> Defines Freud's basic theory of personality structure. W. W. Norton & Co., Inc., 1961.

Fromm, Erich

Escape from Freedom.
>The well-known analyst makes one of the better cases for the argument that man fears freedom. Avon Books, 1971.

Hoffer, Eric

The True Believer.
>The dockhand philosopher describes the strong attraction for people to surrender this freedom for the comfort of being part of a mass movement. Harper & Row, 1951.

Skinner, B. F.

Beyond Freedom and Dignity.
>The most recent statement of the prominent behavioral psychologist that man is not free except in his ability to manipulate his environment.

Sartre, Jean-Paul

Existentialism.
>The direct opposite of the Skinner thesis stating that man is completely free to choose whatever he wants. Philosophical Library, 1947.

CHAPTER FIVE

Bettelheim, Bruno

The Children of the Dream.
>The much-discussed study of Israeli communards in which Bettelheim evaluates the effects of Kubbitz life on children. Avon Books, 1970.

Ellul, Jacques

The Technological Society.
>An overstated case that technology is beyond man's control and the point of departure for arguments on the subject before the Club of Rome filed its report. Random House, Inc.

Galbraith, John Kenneth

The Affluent Society.
>A highly influential book that spelled out just how the United States could be privately affluent and publically poor. Houghton Mifflin, 1971.

The New Industrial State.
>This more recent book locates the new source of power not in land or money but in the "technostructures" of organized corporate systems. Houghton Mifflin, 1971.

Meadows, Donnella H., *et al.*

The Limits of Growth: A Report from the Club of Rome on the Predicament of Mankind.
>The famous doomsday environmental study which champions such things as zero population growth if global disaster is to be averted. Universe Books, Inc., 1972.

Melville, Keith

Communes in the Counter Culture: Origins, Theories, Styles of Life.
A very sympathetic, much too optimistic, but nonetheless interesting view of the communal movement in the United States. Wm. Morrow & Co., 1972.

Mesthene, Emmanuel G.

Technological Change: Its Impact on Man and Society.
A short and informative work stressing the possibility of citizens controlling technological change and of the urgent need to do so. New American Library, 1970.

Schwartz, Eugene S.

Overskill: Technology and the Myth of Efficiency.
A recent, very readable, and highly pessimistic assessment of man's ability to control the technology he has created. Quadrangle Books, 1971.

CHAPTER SIX

Brown, Norman O.

Life Against Death.
Landmark book which extends Freud's theories to suggest that modern man is alienated from his body, that civilization is an unnecessary neurosis, and that the pleasure principle must be asserted to overcome the death instinct. Wesleyan University Press, 1970.

Love's Body.
More of the same, but with greater poetic flourish. (The poetry is still given a scholarly attention which led Theodore Roszach to comment that it is a case of Dionysus with footnotes.) Random House, Inc., 1966.

Cleaver, Eldridge

Soul on Ice.
The Black Panther Information Minister makes a case, among other things, that Black culture has emphasized the body and white culture the mind, and that much could be gained by a coalition between the two. Dell Publishing Co., 1970.

Fromm, Erich

The Forgotten Language.
Speculates on the origins and compares the values of patriarchal and matriarchal societies. Grove Press.

Marcuse, Herbert

Eros and Civilization: A Philosophical Inquiry into Freud.
Like Norman Brown, an argument for the liberation of the pleasure principle in an advanced society. Random House, Inc., 1955.

CHAPTER SEVEN

Cruse, Harold

The Crisis of The Negro Intellectual.
Cruse attempts to demonstrate that America, unlike other countries, does not have a common culture. Wm. Morrow & Co., 1971.

Hall, Edward T.

The Hidden Dimension.
> For Hall, culture is the hidden dimension and he offers some theories on the uses of space and the effect of crowding to measure the way people behave. Doubleday & Co., Inc., 1969.

The Silent Language.
> A cultural anthropologist offers a definition of culture which moves the question to a much deeper level of consciousness, habit, and environmental ethos. Fawcett World Library, 1969.

Novak, Michael

The Rise of the Unmeltable Ethnics; Politics and Culture in the Seventies.
> A prominent Catholic scholar's contribution to the New Pluralism which argues against the melting pot idea and violently attacks the prevailing WASP culture. Macmillan, 1972.

Schrag, Peter

The Decline of the WASP.
> This time a Jewish writer takes up the cudgel against the same foe. Simon & Schuster, 1971.

CHAPTER EIGHT

Braden, William

The Private Sea: LSD and the Search for God.
> The author's exploration of psychedelic drugs, mysticism, and the death of God theology. Quadrangle Books, 1967.

Happold, F. C.

Mysticism: A Study and an Anthology.
> Excellent introduction to mysticism in all its forms and locations around the world as well as a good selection of writings from many mystics. Peter Smith.

James, William

The Varieties of Religious Experience.
> The classic statement by the pioneer American psychologist on the nature of religious experience. Macmillan, 1961.

Marty, Martin E. and Peerman, Dean G.

New Theology Nos. 1 to 9.
> Series which identifies trends in theology by yearly collecting important articles by popular radical theologians. Macmillan, 1964–71.

Northrop, Filmer S.

The Meeting of East and West.
> A comparison of matriarchal and patriarchal social orders plus an excellent explanation of the differences between Eastern and Western metaphysics and possible grounds for reconciliation of the two. Macmillan, 1960.

Ross, Nancy Wilson

The Three Ways of Asian Wisdom: Hinduism, Buddhism, Zen.
> A good general introduction to all major Eastern philosophies. Simon & Schuster, 1968.

CHAPTER NINE

Illich, Ivan D.

Deschooling Society.
> Highly controversial book by a former Catholic priest that calls for the abolition of compulsory education. Harper & Row, 1971.

Jencks, Christopher and Riesman, David.

The Academic Revolution.
> Important and provocative study of the changing dynamics of school systems. Doubleday & Co., Inc. 1968.

Kozol, Jonathan

Death at an Early Age: The Destruction of the Hearts and Minds of Negro Children in the Boston Public Schools.
> An angry but useful analysis of the failure of the educational system in an urban ghetto based on the author's own experience as a teacher in Boston. Bantam Books, Inc., 1970.

Free Schools.
> Kozol's report on the free school movement in which he concedes their failure to teach basic skills—such as how to read. Houghton Mifflin, 1972.

Schwab, Joseph J.

College Curriculum and Student Protest.
> An attempt by a conservative educator to loosen the curriculum practices in colleges by suggesting innovative approaches to providing a good liberal arts background for students. University of Chicago Press, 1970.

CHAPTER TEN

Bell, Daniel

Work and Its Discontents.
> A description of the growing alienation of man from his labor in an industrial society. Beacon Press, 1956.

Freud, Sigmund

Beyond the Pleasure Principle.
> In which Freud considers the death instinct and the limitations of the pleasure principle. This is a source for much of what Marcuse and Brown develop in their later works. Liveright.

Civilization and Its Discontents.
> Freud's analysis of the psychic price man must pay for his civilization with the suggestion that civilization is probably worth the demand. W. W. Norton & Co., Inc., 1962.

Fuller, R. Buckminster

Operating Manual for Spaceship Earth.
    Optimistic, futuristic point for view which sees computerized technology
    eventually creating a super-abundance that will take care of the planet's
    basic problem of not enough to go around. Southern Illinois University Press,
    1969.

Harrington, Michael

Socialism.
    Latest book by the chairman of the Socialist Party who makes a reasoned
    and pragmatic case for democratic socialism which would come with capital-
    ism's failure to make affluence serve broad social needs. Saturday Review
    Press, 1972.

Klausner, Samuel Z., ed.

Why Men Take Chances.
    An anthology of essays examining why men take risks and why stress seems
    to be a necessary ingredient in man's existence. Doubleday & Co., Inc., 1968.

Marcuse, Herbert

One Dimensional Man.
    A highly Germanic Freudian-Marxist version of *Walden* that views consumer-
    ism as the opiate of the masses. A book that has had wide circulation
    within and influence upon the youth movement. Beacon Press, 1964.

Marx, Karl

Capital.
    Still must reading for any informed discussion of social change within a
    capitalistic system. Dutton & Co.

Moltmann, Jurgen

Theology of Hope.
    Future oriented thesis of a European theologian which sees the Kingdom
    of God lying ahead and man's work as the necessary instrument for building
    the kingdom. Harper & Row, 1967.

Teilhard de Chardin, Pierre

How I Believe.

    A short introduction to Teilhard's ideas.

The Future of Man.
    A simpler rendering of the same theme which sees man in a constant state
    of evolution threatened only by the prospect that as man becomes more
    aware of his developing condition, he also becomes more capable of thwarting
    the process. Harper & Row, 1969.

The Phenomenon of Man.
    Teilhard's most complex and most comprehensive attempt to fuse Christian
    dogma with Darwinian evolutionary theory. Harper & Row, 1959.

Weber, Max

The Protestant Ethic and The Spirit of Capitalism.
    Long the central book in any discussion of the value of work because of
    the way Weber connects the Protestant feeling of labor as fulfilling God's
    work on earth and the suitability of that view of the operation of capitalism.
    Charles Scribner's Sons, 1930.

Index

The Family Game
Identities for Young and Old

A television project for the family, produced by WQED Pittsburgh, with a grant from the Corporation for Public Broadcasting, and seen nationally on PBS, the Public Broadcasting Service.
Initial broadcasts: October 1 through December 17, 1972.

Project Directors: Jay Rayvid, Tom Skinner
Executive Producer: John Sommers
Host: Charles Hauck
Group sessions conducted by: Dr. Gerald Edwards, Dr. Lewis Yablonsky
Associate Producers: Scott Larson, Dick Peterson, Paulette Peterson
Television Directors: Tom Cherones, Sam Silberman
Assistants to the Producer: Frank Capuzzi, Susan Marks, Majorie Newman
Production Assistants: Tamsen Merrill, George Morris
Lighting Directors: Carl Augenstein, Al Brennecke
Production Crew: Joseph Abeln, Karen Davis, Azriel Gamliel, Dick Jones, Greg King, Jim Seech, Bill Smales, Mark Stover, Nick Tallo, Frank Warninsky
Technical Supervisor: Dave Hall
Crew Chief: Ken Anderson
Audio: Al Lawyer
Audio Assistants: Merv Lightner, Bob Foreman
Video: Don Williamson
Videotape Editors: Chet Bednar, Don McCall, Robert Millslagle, Bill Moore, Ron Vangura
Camera: Dave Anthony, Dick LaSota, Bob Vaughn, Art Vogel
Set Design: Art Siegel, Lee Waldron
Set Construction: Bob Boley, Harry Meyers
Cinematographer: David Stanton
Sound: Pasquale Buba, John Butler
Design Director: J. Micheal Essex
Additional Film: Denny Carr
Still Photography: Lilo Guest, Bill Hersey, Larry Hitchcock
Advisors:
William Braden, *Chicago Sun-Times*
Dr. Urie Bronfenbrenner, Cornell University
Dr. Sidney Cohen, National Institute of Mental Health
Michael Matthews, M.D., Western Psychiatric Institute
Dr. Helen Nowlis, U.S. Office of Education
Dr. Uvaldo Palomares, Institute for Personal Effectiveness in Children
Dr. Alvin Poussant, Harvard Medical School